Re-reading Poets

PITTSBURGH SERIES IN COMPOSITION,
LITERACY, AND CULTURE

David Bartholomae and Jean Ferguson Carr,
Editors

Re-reading Poets

The Life of the Author

Paul Kameen

University of Pittsburgh Press

Published by the University of Pittsburgh Press, Pittsburgh, Pa., 15260
Copyright © 2011, University of Pittsburgh Press
All rights reserved
Manufactured in the United States of America
Printed on acid-free paper
10 9 8 7 6 5 4 3 2 1

Library of Congress Cataloging-in-Publication Data

Kameen, Paul, 1949–
    Re-reading poets : the life of the author / Paul Kameen.
        p.   cm. — (Pittsburgh series in composition, literacy, and culture)
    Includes bibliographical references and index.
    ISBN-13: 978-0-8229-6107-9 (pbk. : alk. paper)
    ISBN-10: 0-8229-6107-5 (pbk. : alk. paper)
    1. English poetry—History and criticism—Theory, etc. 2. Poetry—Appreciation.
3. Authors and readers. 4. Reader-response criticism. I. Title.
    PR502.K36 2010
    821.009—dc22   2010031523

❦ Contents

> For poetry makes nothing happen: it survives
> In the valley of its making where executives
> Would never want to tamper, flows on south
> From ranches of isolation and the busy griefs,
> Raw towns that we believe and die in; it survives,
> A way of happening, a mouth.
>
> —W. H. Auden, "In Memory of W. B. Yeats"

In the broadest sense, this book is a celebration of the value of poetry and a defense of poetry for our time. Such a defense is not easy to provide in a cultural moment that tends, simultaneously, to think both too much and (as an inevitable consequence of that) too little of poetry: too much, in that its practice and appreciation have been turned over to the experts, the professionals, the poets who write it and the scholars who write *about* it; too little in that few outside of those professional guilds think it has enough to offer toward the living of one's life to pay mind to it in any sustained way. Poetry is afflicted by the same status issues that afflict fine art—we are conditioned to believe that it's a good thing to go and visit it from time to time, in its various museum resting places, but the talents of those who make that art, and the objects they make, seem so far removed from our own lives that mere commemoration (a term I borrow from Martin Heidegger and will come back to from time to time) is our instinctive response.

When I teach the history of literary criticism, I really enjoy the part of the course that deals with the first fifty-five years of the nineteenth century, the heyday of great defenses of poetry: William Wordsworth's elaborate preface to the second edition of *Lyrical Ballads* in 1800; Percy Shelley's soaring tribute to poetic legislation; Ralph Waldo Emerson's rigorous essays on poetry, nature, and experience; John Stuart Mill's lucid essay on the uses of poetry; and Walt Whitman's breathtaking (literally, if you try to read aloud some of those unendingly clipped-up sentences) preface to the first edition of *Leaves of Grass* in 1855. This was a moment when poets were at their cultural apogee, kingpins, not only a restored part of the Republic from which Socrates had so unceremoniously dismissed them a couple of millennia before, but finally running the store. My book is not like these, and can't be, given the present moment. But its spirit and ambitions are the same. Poets, I believe, can and should be collegial partners in our daily living. And my primary evidence of that is they have been partners in mine, from long before I had been schooled in how to read them.

One large question I kept before me as I wrote this book is a simple one: What is poetry good for? That question has a very personal significance for me. Poetry—both in the reading, my primary focus in this book, and the writing, a lifelong avocation of mine—is one of the primary means by which I have established my identity, recorded my history, and encoded my intellectual development, as a purely private matter. It has also been the central axis of my professional life since the day in the middle of my junior year in college when I officially changed my major from physics to English. Reading, writing, and public speaking (the foundational elements for any English teacher) were hard work for me. But they were what I wanted to spend my time with, and doing. And I have.

I bought my first book of poetry in the seventh grade, the *Mentor Book of Major American Poets*, from which I read in bed nightly with great excitement. I try to think now about what made my inner world such a perfect playground for all these poets. And that's how I understood it: I was reading *poets*. I was not, that is, simply engaging with individual poems, texts I might *memorize,* or worse *commemorate*; but rather with these collegial interlocutors who became integral with my actual living *memory* in much the same way that any deeply felt engagement with another person does. I did fancy myself a nascent intellectual and I wanted to act like one. There aren't many real places for a small-town teenager to do that. These poets became interesting partners in that regard.

In addition, I was the kind of person whose head was full of words that raced around colliding with one another nearly senselessly, but with energy, like driverless bumper cars; that slushed up together like crushed ice and then froze into tight, jagged piles; that chattered and then scattered like waves of background static—while I sat in class, worked, even read— a ceaseless, breathing noise that I knew could become useful to me, even creative, if only I could muster it on behalf of something that mattered, and not just to me, but to others who cared deeply about the inner workings of their lives and minds. These poets, and their medium, seemed just the ticket for that. I wanted to get to know them and acted as if I could. I wanted them to get to know me and acted as if they could.

So poetry did make a lot of things happen for me. But this is not a book that hopes to persuade you that poetry should make those same things happen for you. This is not even a book that will try to tell you why you, too, should be reading William Wordsworth, or Samuel Taylor Coleridge, or Walt Whitman, for example (three poets, among many others, I turn and return to to make my case), in the ways that I have. If it were, right there, already, I'd be turning poets into something I have worked mightily to *prevent* them from becoming for me: edifying commodities, something above and beyond, more than I ever was, or worse, important only in an academic way. This book is an attempt to counter that more customary way of reading poetry by recommending another way: not for reading poetry but for reading, and re-reading, poets, these people who invest in their work a seeing, a knowing, a life that invites us not entirely out of our own, which is impossible, or fully into theirs, which is equally impossible, but into an open area between where we can become somehow more and other than ourselves in an ongoing manner. At such points of transaction life and art engage, even merge, in deeply intimate ways.

My method in the book is quite different from most academic treatments of poetry. First of all, this is not a book that seeks to parcel out my scholarly addendum to the formidable body of extant research on the very famous poets I write about, none of whom falls, in any case, into my primary areas of expertise. But it *is* informed in a deep way by scholarship in two specific ways. I have been teaching poetry, among many other things, in college classrooms for over thirty-five years now. Even my most personal writing is inevitably permeated by the preparatory reading I've done for that arena. And, as part of my professional work, I have done some writing on poetry and poetics. An article I wrote about twenty-five years ago, titled "Reading Poets," was in fact the first foray I made into this set of problems, and I borrow its title, with a twist, for this book. I'm sure I would be doing some of this kind of work, for my own purposes, even if I were not an academic. But I am, and that inevitably inflects my thinking about these matters. This is not, though, a book directed primarily to scholars. I choose and then use my sources here in much the same way that I choose and use the poets that are my main focus: as collegial interlocutors, thinkers about matters of this sort that have been helpful to me, more in a conversational way than as supportive authorities. I hope by that means to be able to bring them to some kind of life, as accessible and interesting voices, for readers outside the ivied walls who may have no intrinsic investment in the long-standing arguments about critical matters that those of us on the inside engage in for professional purposes.

There is, though, an argument that I want to make on behalf of the vital role of the author, which happens to be pertinent to where we are currently in the history of literary criticism. Those of us who read and teach literature for a living have an obvious stake in its implications. But even those who would never open such books are affected by them, primarily by the way in which reading and writing get taught in the schools. For nearly a century now, the figure of the author has been diminished or dismissed or margin-alized or depersonalized by the dominant critical ideologies, first by text-based systems (especially, in America, the New Criticism) and then by the variety of more recent reader-based systems that I'll broadly congregate un-der the umbrella term of postmodernism. There was a lot to be said to fully elucidate T. S. Eliot's injunction—made in 1920 as he looked around at the wreckage of the previous century's predominantly author-based approaches to critical reading—that "[h]onest criticism and sensitive appreciation is directed not upon the poet but upon the poetry" (*SW* 53). I want to say something now toward balancing the equation. So a part of my ambition is to re-animate the figure of the author, the poet, as an active force, a "person-ality," if you will (to violate one of Eliot's injunctions), even a "vital" "pres-ence," (to interject terms that are anathema to two different strands of more recent critical theory), in the interpretive process. My hope is that, insider-sounding as some of this material might seem, I will have done enough in the telling—especially in my discussion of the poets who are my argument's foundation—to prevent this facet of the book from being too off-putting for readers outside of my profession, the broader audience I want to engage.

This is not a book that scripts an agenda for how to teach poetry. It is, though, in two specific ways, very much a book about teaching. I will talk a lot about how poets can and do teach their readers things about life that are of considerable import. All of the poets I write about, all of the poets I've ever read, I'd dare say, have taught me something of consequence. What I especially like about my primary subjects is that they actually carve out, in a variety of ways, specific positions for us to stand in as potential learners, thereby making ourselves eligible for the knowledge and wisdom they proffer. Without this kind of pre- and extra-academic learning as a foundation, I would not be able to even imagine, let alone strive toward, the sort of teaching and learning I want to foster in the classroom. Most English teachers would, I believe, say much the same thing about how their own reading informs in a tacit way the whys and hows of their teaching. I also want to call attention to this kind of teaching, which is foundational to the one that issues from certified expertise. It constitutes what I have called elsewhere the "position of the teacher" (*WT* 138), which derives not so much from disciplinary knowledge, but from the lifelong lending of ourselves to the teacherly voices we most admire, especially the ones we encounter in our reading, until their values and ambitions become integral with our own. It is such a position that *prepares* those of us who end up in front of literature classrooms to do something that we would not otherwise be capable of doing: bringing poets' lives into an intimate relationship with the lives of the students sitting in front of us, these readers who might not be inclined at the outset to imagine that such a relationship is even possible, let alone profitable in a deep and lifelong manner. This position is similarly available to readers of poets who are not being paid to teach. It allows us to share the knowledge and wisdom we gain from such reading with anyone in our company—a spouse, a child, a friend, a colleague—who is willing to listen and respond. In other words, teaching, like poetry, belongs to all of us and is useful, I would say, at least as much outside of school as it is within.

In a similar way, once we begin to read a poet *as* a poet, we inevitably begin to read *like* a poet, not simply with an eye toward the knowledge or wisdom that individual poems proffer, valuable as that certainly is, nor even with an ear toward writing poems of our own, appealing as that might be, but with a gathering awareness, through extended reading and re-reading, of how a specific poet promulgates a unique "life" in such a way that we can be changed by it. Poets can provide us with such a wide variety of experiences, very much like our own firsthand experiences, far beyond what it is possible to acquire in a single human lifetime. The method of reading I propose invites us to be poets in our own right, whether or not we choose to write our own poems.

On balance, despite the fact that I have devoted much of my intellectual and emotional energy to poetry over the years, I'm inclined to side with Auden on the "happening" aspect of poetry: Many things may happen because of poetry, but poetry does not "make" them happen. One of the great values of poets is that, in the process of trying to tell some true things, they are largely satisfied to let you alone to make happen what you want to make happen and with their help can make happen. I have that ambition when I write my own poems and I have a similar ambition in the work I am doing here. But I also want to call attention to the last line of my epigraph, where the term "happen" appears the second time, in a new form, as a "way" and, to complete the series of river metaphors that holds this stanza together, as a "mouth." I like those ways of conceiving happening, as in a happening onto something along the way, as in what inevitably happens when a river runs its full course, delivering, finally, what it has carried for so long from its open mouth, as, simply, what "survives." The poets I write about here have accompanied me quite companionably along my way and have opened a mouth that allows me to speak in my own words—through theirs, as the residual tradition in which I operate—what I would be otherwise incapable of saying.

In its material terms, this book is a telling from my point of view of the value a number of specific poets have had for me as peers, friends, colleagues; they come in when I invite them to help me think about something, cope with something, or just get through the day. Much of my commentary on these poets will come to life more immediately, of course, for those who have already at some point read from their work. But that is not a pre-requisite. My ultimate intention is to offer a method of re-reading as an inducement for you to add a poet or two that interests *you*—perhaps one you remember having liked at some point for your own personal reasons, perhaps one you'll encounter down the road—to the other kinds of authors you turn to more regularly to help you engage with culture, history, tradition, and, especially, your own everyday life in meaningful ways. That's where all the personal stories I end up telling come in. These may have about them, in isolation, the sound and feel of memoir. And they are that. But the real purpose of that material is as evidence, as illustration, of the *kinds* of things that this sort of a reading practice brings to the fore: the life that is being lived, in a deep and enduring way, in intimate concert with the life of the author. It is only by this means—by becoming enmeshed with a reader's everyday life—that an author *can* come to life in a meaningful way, as is the case with any real relationship. Same thing for the scholarly material: It's there because it's an integral part of my experience as a reader, which doesn't mean it's necessary to *do* this kind of research to enjoy poets in the ways I have or to enjoy this book.

The book is organized into four chapters, each designed as a sustained meditation on one broad theme or question (which I announce at the outset) pertinent to my overall argument. Such concepts—chapters, theme, argument—apply here in only their loosest sense. The book moves in an unusual way, one that is hard to describe beforehand and that I hope will not seem too disjunctive or disorderly to readers accustomed to, well, unitary chapters with precise themes and progressively staged arguments. Rather than speaking from a univocal, authorial position, I deploy by turns a range of disparate discourses: critical theory, autobiography, history of philosophy, close reading, memoir, course materials, scholarship, all turning into, toward, and away from one another in a staccato fashion. I anoint none of them as ultimately authoritative. It is by their juxtaposition with one another, as a matter of method, that my own re-reading project has advanced for me personally and can, I believe, advance a comparable re-reading project for other readers. The book, in other words, enacts the mode of re-reading it recommends.

The first chapter explores a fundamental literary critical matter: the role and place of the author as a personal force in readerly transactions. I examine an excerpt from I. A. Richards's *Practical Criticism* (1929) that, to me, announces the exile of the author from our critical discourses and I then document the historical aftermath of that gesture. The rest of the chapter details a method of reading that I have been using since I first started reading poems on my own, which presumes both commonality and collegiality between poet and reader. I rely on my long-term experiences as a reader of Wordsworth, Coleridge, Whitman, and T. S. Eliot, along with an extended discussion of imagism, to outline the basic assumptions of this approach to reading poets.

The next chapter explores temporality in a local, narrow way, as it applies psychologically to the individual lives of my subject poets and to me as a persistent reader of their work. The problem of how one achieves individual identity over time, through writing and reading, is at the center of my concern here. I engage in detail with three major poems: Wordsworth's "Ode: Intimations of Immortality," Coleridge's "The Rime of the Ancient Mariner," and Whitman's "Song of Myself," focusing in particular on how these poets use the metaphor of the "soul" to reflect on matters of personal identity; and I examine several poets I was reading simultaneously at a crucial point in my own development during the 1960s.

The third chapter explores time in a much broader context: how we engage, as readers, with the past via the "tradition," which preprocesses important texts in ways that often make it difficult for us to connect directly with their authors. I consider an excerpt from my freshman writing course description and then branch off to discuss various approaches for conceptualizing history and, more generally, temporality, relying on figures like T. S. Eliot, Martin Heidegger, and especially Mikhail Bakhtin as vehicles for my inquiry. Once again, my three primary poets, some literary history (in this case, the evolution of image-based poetry in the twentieth century), as well as autobiographical stories, elaborate my case. I conclude the chapter with a long examination of my own thirty-year readerly history with the work of the Greek poet/philosopher Parmenides to illustrate the role of re-reading in the process of recovering a poet from the tradition.

The last chapter explores both the public and the private aspects of the question of who gets to be a poet and how, if at all, that is related to the process of actually writing poems. John Stuart Mill is my framing thinker here. I examine the notion of "originality" as it applies to poetic production; I detail the process of my own evolution as a poet (and not-poet); and I conclude with an argument on behalf of poetry as a means to an end that is beyond the poetic rather than as an end in itself.

The epilogue offers a few of my own poems, written over the last thirty years, as well as some context for the sort of creative enterprise I've engaged in myself, as part of my contribution to the ongoing conversation with all these poets.

Re-reading Poets

One ❧ The Life of the Author

I READ THE POETS THAT CONCERN ME most in this book both before and while I became a practicing professional myself, over a long period of time. The advantage of this is that I have come to understand in a direct way the ultimately casual and temporary nature of the critical preferences that happen to be currently dominant and the modes of reading they promote. Criticism, it is clear to anyone who practices it over more than a generation or so, is always a historically produced, and therefore ideological, construction with a definable (in retrospect at least) life cycle (a period of gestation, a period of production, and a period of decline). It is all too easy, from outside the institutional matrix that generates and promulgates critical ideologies, to be blind to these machinations and to erroneously presume that the practices in vogue at the moment are in fact the natural ones by which humans are meant to process literary texts or, if not that, a better set than any of the recent competitors. While there may be no way to get fully outside of whatever happens to be the currently dominant system, we do not have to follow its precepts docilely and blindly. History is replete with alternatives to the currency at hand. My course description for a History of Criticism seminar says this explicitly: "So, no matter how dominant the current critical system might seem to be, it is necessarily temporary, in process, always already well on its way to being replaced by the next new thing, before we even finish thinking and talking about it." I have comparable language in my entry-level Critical Reading course description. Such statements get at what I see as the crux of the problem both of what poets have to teach and how they help us to learn it.

The whole system of "close reading," for example, which dominated the way I learned in school to approach poetry, remained largely invisible to me (as system, that is) while I learned to practice it. That I found the way school read poets so boring and unprofitable, from early in my high school years and on through my college years was typical (everyone else in my classes did, too, as far I could tell) and understandable, given the difficulty of the method and the quotidian tedium of the environment. The fact that it didn't ruin poets as figures of lifelong value for me was due to the happy accident that I started to read them before we began to study poetry in earnest. And I had already come up with another way of doing it.

It is not impossible to privately ignore the dominant system and cobble together a more agreeable alternative. It is, though, hard to become conscious of the current system as system—to see it in a broadly orchestral historical frame, as one option among many that are comparably powerful. From this perspective one can become vigilant to the potential limitations and excesses of criticism's constitutive practices not simply at the transitional junctures, when the extant system begins to fray and fall apart as it is being replaced by a contrary alternative—all the seams become quite visible, then—but during the heydays, when the machine is powerful, seemingly faultless, and almost universally endorsed. One way to reach such a consciousness is to be around when one of the sea changes takes place. In the case of literary criticism, such upheavals took place in the 1920s (when text-based theories began to emerge) and the 1970s (when reader-based theories began to replace them), among others. Since the original and previously presumed-to-be natural system remains, in a sort of disabled state of partial erasure, as the new system replaces it, the duplicity of theory is forever exposed. One can, then, begin to study such ideological movements from a sort of anthropological perspective, which is what I'd like to do a bit of next: a quick sketch of one aspect of the last eighty years of critical theories and the methods of reading they promoted: the way the author, the poet, was sent to the sidelines of the reading process.

In 1929, I. A. Richards published *Practical Criticism,* in which he described this technique for teaching poetry:

> For some years I have made the experiment of issuing printed sheets of poems—ranging in character from a poem by Shakespeare to a poem by Ella Wheeler Wilcox—to audiences who were requested to comment freely in writing upon them. The authorship of the poems was not revealed, and with rare exceptions it was not recognised.
>
> After a week's interval I would collect these comments, taking certain obvious precautions to preserve the anonymity of the commentators, since only through anonymity could complete liberty to express their genuine opinions be secured for the writers. . . . I lectured the following week partly upon the poem, but rather more upon the comments, or protocols, as I call them.
>
> Much astonishment both for the protocol-writers and for the Lecturer ensued from this procedure. (3–4)

The feeling of both anxious bafflement and sudden power—which may be what Richards means by "astonishment" here—that these various anonymous protocol-writers (the majority of whom "were undergraduates reading English with a view to an Honors Degree" in Richards's class) must have experienced, in the mid-1920s, when first confronted by the similarly anonymous poems before them would be hard, I think, for us to imagine, let alone replicate, inured as we are by three generations of critical theory to a way of reading that valorizes text or reader over author as the dominant matrix of a poem's meaning and merit. Most likely their first key to reading a poem for academic purposes would have been to look at the author's name and then use it to cue into any number of ready-made discourses for casting responses in biographical, historical, or formulary terms. The nineteenth century was rife with such approaches to reading poets. One can see ample evidence of these predilections in the protocols that Richards excerpts for us in the first part of his book. There is, for example, the occasional guess at authorial provenance, or a quick recognition of form or genre, that allows a student-reader to regain a familiar critical purchase. And the overall tenor of the protocols, ranging by turns from the generically bland to the vaguely laudatory to the snidely dismissive suggest how well these student-writers had memorized the moods and moves of contemporaneous criticism.

Richards's simple classroom "procedure" certainly signals toward, in a most efficient way, what has been a century-long process of de-author-izing poetic criticism. Only in retrospect, though, does the excerpt from Richards seem meaningful in the way I have indicated. Richards had, at that time, as far as I can tell, no express project to dismantle author-based approaches to reading and writing. He seems himself hardly to notice, let alone follow up on, the novelty of his removing authors' names from their poems in his classroom. He makes no overt argument on behalf of this move as a counterweight to the author- or intention-oriented criticisms that dominated his day. He promotes his system simply as "new"—a "new kind of documentation," a "new technique"—which is the adjective that ultimately stuck to the mode of criticism his work helped to engender: the text-based method of reading that he and his British colleagues developed and exported to us, in America, to elaborate into the New Criticism (the capital letters provided by John Crowe Ransom's 1941 book of that title) over the next thirty years or so.

The rest of Richards's book is more an argument for a case-based, quasi-scientific approach to the study of student reading strategies and practices that are grounded in the sort of induction that the field of psychology was using to establish itself in disciplinary terms. Had the intellectual drift of the moment been slightly different, Richards's work might now be viewed not through the lens of the emergent text-based economy of critical reading (thus allowing me to make a big deal here out of what is, in his book, really only a passing remark about his technique) but through the lens of the reader-based approach that is also nascent in his work (especially in *Practical Criticism*), which did not emerge fully for a couple of generations. Louise Rosenblatt, for example, was, roughly, a contemporary of Richards. Her now-iconic book, *Literature as Exploration*, which helped to launch the reader-response movement in this country in the 1970s, was first published in 1938, less than a decade after *Practical Criticism*. But by then the momentum already had swung so strongly in favor of a text-based ideology that her voice would not be heard in any deeply resonant way for three decades.

In 1954, right around the time I was starting to read, Richards's simple gesture achieved its ultimate critical mandate, when William K. Wimsatt and Monroe Beardsley posited that the poem "is not the critic's own and not the author's" (750). Authorial intentions—whether express or tacit—are thereby exiled to the far outskirts of the interpretive process, as are the critic's affects. With reader and writer suitably disengaged from their immediate personal or historical circumstances, what remains is the text, which provides an "internal" evidence of its own by means of which its significance can be "discovered" through an examination of the "semantics and syntax" that are the poem's "public" face (753). These "intentional" and "affective" "fallacies," having been in the marketplace less ostentatiously for a number of years, and as unnamed initiatives for much longer, were finally established as methodological linchpins for the New Criticism.

The progress away from the author that Richards signals in *Practical Criticism* reaches its apogee—one that Richards himself would likely be aghast at—just about forty years after his first classroom experiment, with Roland Barthes's landmark essay "The Death of the Author," first published in 1968, the year after I graduated from high school. Barthes does not make the concept of *an* author irrelevant to the activity of reading. Nor does Foucault shortly after him, in his comparably influential essay "What Is an Author?" which gave us the soon ubiquitous concept of the "author function." What Barthes is concerned about is *the* Author, with a capital A, that antecedent force of imaginative creation, invented figurally by processes of commodification and canonization, and then rendered literally through successive acts of autobiography, biography, and explanation. He says: "To give a text an Author is to impose a limit on that text, to furnish it with a final signified, to close the writing. Such a conception suits criticism very well, the latter then allotting itself the important task of discovering the Author (or its hypostases: society, history, psyche, liberty) beneath the work: when the Author has been found, the text is 'explained'—victory to the critic" (147).

I don't think there are many among us these days who want to resurrect that particular version of the relationship between Author and critic. But death is a serious and final matter, and I'm beginning to think that in the case of the author, Barthes's eulogy, Wimsatt and Beardsley's fallacy, and even Richards's simple elision were overstated. This is certainly so for the many poets I have spent my time re-reading, especially for the ones that have come most fully to life for me, as colleagues and friends, over the course of my life. The three poets to whom I will turn most often to make my case, William Wordsworth, Samuel Taylor Coleridge, and Walt Whitman, happened to enter my readerly life earlier than the others, before I "learned" how to read them in school, through the regimen of the New Criticism, which was how *I* first experienced the "death" of my authors.

Oddly enough, most of the American New Critics, those formidable theorists who seemed hell-bent on winching poetry away from the easy reach of casual readers, were themselves practicing poets. What could their motivation have been for such a seemingly self-defeating

agenda? We need to delve a little deeper into the background and history of the movement to begin to make sense of this apparent contradiction. The critical apparatus for a text-based approach to poetry was
being assembled in the 1920s, as modernism began to clamber up from
the shambles of post–World War I Europe, primarily through the work
of an array of British theorists who were *not* poets: I. A. Richards, C. K.
Ogden, F. R. Leavis, and William Empson most prominent among them.

At the same time, a group of "Fugitive Poets" was organizing itself at
Vanderbilt University in Tennessee: John Crowe Ransom, Allen Tate, Don-
ald Davidson, and Robert Penn Warren were the most notable, but there
were others, all with deep roots, at least initially, in Southern regionalist poetics. The primary organ of the group was their literary magazine, the *Fugitive*, which they published between 1922 and 1925. The aesthetic of the group
was relatively austere, with an emphasis on craft and an aversion for sentimentality. But there was a much less visible cultural agenda here as well,
promulgated by the Southern Agrarians, a movement that evolved from the
Fugitive Poets and included all of the poets I mention above, among others. Their manifesto, *I'll Take My Stand: The South and the Agrarian Tradition*, by "12 Southerners," was published in 1930. The various essays in the
book promote a critique of American industrialism—quite an astute, radical, and cogent critique—offering as an alternative the traditional agrarian
values of the Old South. One senses throughout this book the deep-seated,
sometimes seething resentments of the Reconstruction era, a comparably
deep-seated longing for a romanticized version of the antebellum South.
The writers advocated a return to a traditional, land- and farming-based
economy as a counter to the rootlessness and dehumanization of Northern,
urban modernity. The politics underlying the system are consonant in many
ways with traditional conservatism, organized as they are around regional-
ism, individualism, and anti-Communism. Tate even wanted the book to
be titled *Tracts against Communism*. There are faint traces of racism here and
there, an occasional hint toward the Lost Cause of the Confederacy. But
these are more residual than central elements of the ideology.

What, if anything, could this possibly have to do with reading poetry?
Well, for one thing, it imagines the ideal reader of a poem as a solitary reflective, spending considerable time in the evening, at leisure, ruminating
patiently on great, ennobling texts, difficult texts that need to be savored,
circulated through and around, repeatedly if necessary, until they yield their
harvest. This may not be rendered in the book expressly as a plantation-
based idyll, but it's certainly not a sharecropper's version of the agrarian life

either. What better method for insulating poetry from the vast, busy masses of the hectic workforce in the North than a method of close reading that required time, stability, pedigree, "cultivation," the very odd sort of populist elitism that emerged more generally from a nostalgia for a world gone with the wind? Most of the poets in this group are not inordinately complex or dense. Some are quite accessible. But it was their political inclinations—even when they were at odds with their economic interest in reaching a broad audience, or even with their aesthetic—that seem to me to have led them to their critical conclusions. That a couple of generations of us had to learn to read poems according to this regimen is an interesting historical sidelight. And looked at that way, it argues precisely for an awareness of the historically contingent nature not only of critical theories but also of the seemingly more benign modes of reading they engender and that we tend to adopt without too much question. The agenda of the Southern Agrarians was largely overwritten by subsequent theorists such as Cleanth Brooks, the chief architect and exemplar of the New Critical method, whose work (some of it written in concert with Penn Warren) dominated criticism and pedagogy in English into the 1960s. In fact, by the time most critical ideologies arrive in the classroom, their politics have been pretty much bleached out. Which is a whole different thing from saying they were never there in the first place.

IN 1883, DECADES BEFORE RICHARDS was tinkering with poems in his classroom, Olive Schreiner wrote in *The Story of an African Farm:* "But there is another method—the method of life we all lead. Here nothing can be prophesied. There is a strange coming and going of feet. Men appear, act and react upon each other, and pass away" (29). I came across her work while I was writing my dissertation on John Berryman, who borrows the first phrase from this passage—"But there is another method"—as one of the epigraphs of his *Dream Songs* (385). Schreiner calls the first method the "stage method," wherein "characters and their actions are completely subject to the overall aesthetic intent. They are always secondary to the logic of form, pre-determined, as it were, to follow out their courses in preconceived and predictable ways" (29). Berryman is clearly interested in writing poems orchestrated by "life," with its "strange coming and going of feet," rather than "aesthetic intent," "preconceived and predictable."

I bring this up here for two reasons: First of all, I want to start laying out "another method" for reading poets, using, roughly, a comparable distinction between "life" and "stage." But there's an equally important second matter that needs to be accounted for in the process: the role and status of the author in this transaction, a matter made problematic enough to require another method simply because so much of what I do as a reader of poets, and want to recommend, flies in the face of the previous century's critical dynamic. In order for me to make the case I want to make on behalf of the "poet" as the complementary agent in a dyadic relationship, I have to find a way to re-involve the author in some sort of personal role in the dynamic of reading.

The relationships I have had over the years with the poets I will be discussing (though I could quite agreeably generalize this to include many, many others) have been as deep, full, complex, and durable as relationships I've had with actual people. The whole way of thinking about human relationships that sharply distinguishes those that are putatively actual from those that are merely textual makes no sense to me any longer, at least not in its most rigorous, commonsensical form. In some respects, I feel I have become better at getting to know the actual people present to me as complex and interesting in a deeply meaningful way *because* I've been able to develop such relationships with the absent poets who interest me. To be sure, the poets on the other side of their poems are my own concoctions, they can change drastically over time, and they often have only the barest connection to their biographical versions, which I knew almost nothing about at the outset in any case and have not taken undue pains to find out about in the meantime. But is this that much different, really, from the actual relationships we develop, where our "reading" of the other is often grounded in the barest bits of discourse and is refracted through an assortment of prior desires, needs, expectations, preferences, models, biases, and categories—sometimes personal, sometimes social, sometimes cultural—that pre-construct the other for us and over which we tend to assert very little conscious control? Getting past, or just seeing more clearly through, those prisms, to the extent that it's possible, requires work and time, patience, and care, even imagination: a mode of reading and re-reading, I would argue, akin to the one I propose here for these other "others." One way to define it, for both realms, is as "living conversation," a term I borrow from Mikhail Bakhtin. In living conversation, we seek not *primarily* to decode our interlocutor's "meaning" (as formalist approaches to reading tend to do), nor *primarily* to produce an appropriate "response" (as more recent approaches tend to do), but to hear a voice speaking and to listen to it in such a way that it "provokes an answer" (280).

As a teenager, during the time I was getting to know these poets for the first or second time, I spent huge tracts of time—an average, I'd guess now, of three or four hours a day—at a local hangout called The Sugar Bowl. It was the kind of place memorialized now in nostalgic treatments of the 1950s. For me, it was a most redeeming diversion from the otherwise featureless panoramas of the vast savanna of my adolescence. There were about eight high-back booths, a few tables, a counter with stools, anywhere from three to thirty people there at a time. I'd go up after dinner, camp out at one of those spots, by myself, just drinking coffee and thinking whatever I felt like thinking; then I'd shift to another and another spot over the course of the evening and just talk to people—about anything from school gossip to the existence of God. Thinking back now, I believe that it was because I was reading all these poets that I could and did imagine that everyone I interacted with, these collegial interlocutors, was animated by the same potential for living conversation, if only I could find ways to initiate it. I have the same feeling to this day, this welling up of excitement about the possibilities of sustained intellectual relationship, when I walk into a class on the first day, especially an entry-level class where the faces—that pleasant combination of (inspiring) hope for something great to happen and (challenging) deep skepticism that it can in such a venue—remind me of the faces I looked forward to encountering in The Sugar Bowl. Not all of those encounters went great. Some were painful and boring. Same now. But the fact that I can still feel a surge of motivation at such moments, well, that derives at least as much from my having read these poets as it does from any institutional structures I'm familiar with, or from my own moral fiber.

❧

TO BE HONEST, I JUST CAN'T FIGURE OUT retrospectively why I started to read the poets who have accompanied me for over forty-five years when I first did, in my early teens. There is nothing leading up to it that can account for or explain this sudden, deep fascination poetry held for me. I do recall having to memorize a poem to recite to the class in the second grade. Mine was Tennyson's "The Brook."

> I come from haunts of coot and hern,
> I make a sudden sally,
> And sparkle out among the fern,
> To bicker down a valley.

I'm pretty sure that these lines I quote, from memory, are that poem's opening lines. When my turn came, I went to the front of the room, stood stiff as a board, and said my poem out as fast as I could, robotically, monotonically. Mrs. Zebrosky, my favorite elementary school teacher, chided me about that. I went back and sat down. That's what I knew about poetry—all of it bad, really, both the sing-songy poem and the embarrassment of my enactment of it—for most of my childhood. Then, all of sudden, five years later, I bought a book of poems and started reading them every night before I went to bed, secretly, memorizing poem after poem, reciting the lines over and over silently in my head. It was fantastic. And a big part of that had to do with the fact that it had nothing whatsoever to do with school. Until I got to high school, my English courses were almost entirely grammar-oriented. Year after year of it. I liked it. It was like math, which I was good it. I still diagram sentences in my head. But the main value of this was that I got to read poetry, and develop my own way for reading poets, for a couple of years without any intrusion from school. When we finally started reading literature in high school, the "day" poets I came across there seemed to have little to do with the "night" poets I spent my own time with, even when, from time to time, they went by exactly the same names. The ones at school became knowledge for me in much the same way that Tennyson's poem did. I memorized what I had to in order to recite it back in tests. The ones at home proffered knowledge of a much different order and kind, and I read them in an entirely different way because of that.

While reading my poets outside the institutional and disciplinary confines of school, I had a very specific idea in mind, an agenda, if you will, for what they would provide me. I honestly now, looking back, have no idea how I came up with the assumptions that guided my process. But they were very clear to me and I believed in them adamantly. First of all, as I framed out my overall project, its primary purpose was to broaden and deepen the range of my personal experience. I grew up in a small town in a typical family. I concluded that in my ordinary course of transit through my actual everyday life I could accumulate a limited number and only certain kinds of experiences, on the basis of which I could engender only a limited amount and only certain kinds of knowledge and wisdom. I wanted to think and feel simultaneously across as broad a spectrum as possible. The prism of my personal life could only deliver the visible light portion of that spectrum. I just knew, again for reasons I can't account for retrospectively, that there were something like the X-rays further down on one end and the radio waves further up on the other end, and I wanted to tune myself to that extended range of frequencies.

Poetry, when I found it, looked to me like the perfect vehicle for that. I simply started to read the poets I liked in the ways that seemed comfortable and compelling to me, and on the basis of those practices, something that might fairly be called a "method," this other method, emerged. The fact that most of those early practices, by happenstance, turned out (I later discovered) to be contrary to the general academic assumptions, at that historical moment, about the distinctive nature of poetic discourse may not be entirely coincidental, but it is certainly incidental. When I came later to study poetry in school under the more rigorous regime of the watered-down version of the New Criticism that informed most high school textbooks, I was a little taken aback by how mystifying it tended to make what had come to seem to me quite straightforward and simple.

The school approach, for example, assumed that poetry was hard to understand and difficult to read. My experience had already told me that, at least with the poets I was reading, quite the contrary was true. Poetry was no harder to read than anything else. It actually seemed much easier because poems were quite short relative to other kinds of creative and academic texts. And on a material level they were easier to assimilate. Rhythm, rhyme, and meter seemed to me to organize the reading experience in quite amenable ways, facilitating, even speeding up, the reading process.

The school approach assumed that the meanings of poetry were "hidden" within, or even "behind," the surface of the poem and that they had to be ferreted out with a set of almost surgically precise critical instruments. My own experience had been quite the opposite: I felt that the poets I was reading were talking to me very casually, personally, openly, clearly, as if we were in the same room together, conversing. And the deep and immediate emotional and physical impact they had on me made me believe that poetic discourse was the most direct kind of verbal medium available, one which actually did carry the full weight of its meaning very efficiently right on the surface.

The school approach assumed that poems needed to be read slowly, assiduously. My own experience indicated that, at least initially, while I was getting a feel for the potential relationship to be developed with a poet, speed was the key. Read fast, read a lot, get into the poet's inner workings, the rhythms of thinking, and ride them out into the worlds they engender. I strove toward the (then seemingly) impossible dream of absorbing a whole poem in an instant of time, at the speed of life as it were, just like lived sensation.

The differences here are not merely matters of technique. There are fundamental differences at the epistemic level, in terms of the nature and kind of knowledge a poet might be proffering and the manner in which it will be received. What I got from reading poets was a kind of experience that had significant status, comparable in many ways to my own and quite different from what I got from reading, say, a textbook or watching TV. I felt I was migrating into someone else's position without losing my own: a peculiar kind of interanimation.

♣

A FEW YEARS AGO I WAS USING a sequence of assignments for my freshman writing course that revolved around the concept of "experience." The opening-day diagnostic assignment, which we use in my department to get a writing sample and make certain limited kinds of decisions about course placement, basically asked students to question, then reflect and comment upon, the commonplace: "Experience is the best teacher." During the time period I used this assignment, I probably read a hundred responses. They were all over the place, but they shared one thing: a very sharp divide between firsthand experience—life lessons, street-smarts, hard knocks, gut feelings, etc.—and book learning—school lessons, book smarts, ivory tower, logic, etc. A student might value one side somewhat or dramatically more than the other or both equally, but the difference between them was strict and strictly enforced. This was to be expected. The assignment almost invited it, as the course assignments thereafter invited many kinds of interrogations and complications of this underlying symmetry. The surprising thing to me was that, by the end of the course, while many students had in fact written pieces that demonstrated in one way or another that the difference between the kind of knowledge one acquires from reading and the kind one acquires from everyday living were not entirely distinct and separable species, very few of them seemed willing or able to expressly break the spell of the initial dichotomy they started with on day one.

In the *Meno,* Plato offers one wedge for working into, if not breaking, that spell.

> SOCRATES: . . . If someone knows the way to Larissa, or anywhere
> else you like, then when he goes there and takes others with him
> he will be a good and capable guide, you would agree?
> MENO: Of course.

SOCRATES: But if a man judges correctly which is the road, though
he has never been there and doesn't know it, will he not also
guide others aright?

MENO: Yes, he will.

SOCRATES: And as long as he has a correct opinion on the points
about which the other has knowledge, he will be just as good a
guide, believing the truth but not knowing it.

MENO: Just as good. (381, 97a–b)

In general, for a teacher, Socrates prefers the guide who knows the way
(has knowledge) over the guide with a good sense of direction (has correct
opinion). But what about those things that "cannot be taught"? For these
"knowledge is not the guide" (383, 99b). Virtue, for example, says Socrates,
is not a form of knowledge and "will be acquired neither by nature nor by
teaching. Whoever has it gets it by divine dispensation" (383, 100a).

I want to take some liberties with Socrates' paradigm and use his concepts—knowledge, correct opinion, divine dispensation—in a loose way
to think about the problem of just what sort of experience poets translate
over to us through their works. You can, for example, imagine a poet simply as a guide you recruit to get you to Larissa, one who has been there before, and you just go along for the ride. Certainly, simply sitting back and
following a knowledgeable guide is a very good way to get to Larissa. But
there is the nagging implication (even in this dialogue, though Socrates
resists it) that in tagging along this way, you will arrive at your destination
without any understanding of how to (or any confidence that you could, at
some later time) make the trip on your own. Or you can imagine a guide
who, though not having been to Larissa and therefore not knowing the
exact route, appears nonetheless to have a good enough sense of direction
to get on the right track, identify the right landmarks, lead the way, and
arrive with you there in the end. With this second type of guide, you will
be more likely to get involved in the process, thereby learning a way to Larissa and, perhaps, even learning something about finding your way more
generally.

One set of metaphors for characterizing this distinction is destination
vs. journey, and, as it happens, that is roughly the one that Coleridge uses in
his *Biographia Literaria* to differentiate poetry from other kinds of writing.
He says that, in a poem, "The reader should be carried forward, not merely
or chiefly by the mechanical impulse of curiosity, or by a restless desire to

arrive at the final solution; but by the pleasurable activity of mind excited by the attractions of the journey itself" (149).

There is no better place to start thinking about this idea of journey than with Coleridge's masterpiece "The Rime of the Ancient Mariner," most of which is devoted to the old sailor's recounting, to a very recalcitrant listener, of his voyage as a young man into (heroically) and then back from (horrifically) the great Southern Ocean. The poem also, conveniently, offers a simple template for thinking about the various levels of experience I talked about above and who gets to learn what from whom.

The mariner, as a young deckhand, certainly took the full trip to his own Larissa. His off-the-cuff slaying of an albatross leads to a dreadful sequence of afflictions at the hand of "the lonesome Spirit from the south-pole" (526, line 380): first for the ship's crew which, slowly dying from thirst on the painting-still ocean, is finally claimed by "DEATH," who rides in on a spectral skeleton-ship; then for him, as he is forced to live on under the torturous spell of "The Night-mare LIFE-IN-DEATH" (523, 189–93), who wins him in a dice throw. All manner of suffering is inflicted upon him on his spirit-guided journey home; and once he arrives, fully traumatized, he is gripped by a compulsion to tell his story to the hermit and the other two men who drag him out of the drink. Clearly, this is a man who has learned something from his "experience," been utterly devastated and transformed, really, by his journey. "Since then," he says, "at an uncertain hour, / That agony returns," and he must "teach" his tale again and again to "the man who must hear me" (528, 583–90). In this iteration, the mariner is now old and gray, and the man who must hear his tale is a "wedding guest" heading for church, whom the mariner waylays. The wedding guest is straitlaced and impatient (qualities I shared with him when I started reading this poem and have worked hard to mitigate, sometimes with the help of this poem, over the forty-some years since). No way he wants to sit through this story, especially if it means missing the wedding "feast;" and he is highly unlikely, it seems at the outset, to learn anything from it. Yet, by poem's end, having been caught under the mariner's spell, having thereby taken a version of the mariner's journey, "A sadder and a wiser man / he rose the morrow morn" (529, 624–25). I will talk more in chapter 2 about what he seems to have learned from all this forced listening. But one of the clear purposes of the mariner's work was to help his listener avoid a fate comparable to his own. And one of the clear effects of his telling is that the wedding guest has at least a general idea of what he needs to do to avoid such a torturous trip. In other words, he gets the "experience" of going to a pretty horrible Larissa without all the physical tribulations that the mariner had to endure. That's something of value.

But what, if any, wisdom, one might fairly ask, do we as readers acquire by taking our journey through the poem that dramatizes the interaction between the mariner and the wedding guest? About a month ago, I taught this poem in an entry-level literature class for non-majors. After we finished, I asked the class whether they thought the mariner had learned something of consequence from his firsthand experience. Everyone raised a hand. I asked them whether they thought the wedding guest had learned something of consequence from simply hearing the story. Everyone raised a hand. I asked them then which type of learning of such a lesson did they prefer. Everyone preferred to learn from hearing about rather than actually living through the nightmarish experience. Finally, I asked them how many of them felt they had learned something comparable to the wedding guest simply by reading the poem. Only a smattering raised a hand quickly, a few more than that halfheartedly, less than half the class in all. So, if you prefer to learn from someone else's experience, making it a part of your own, but don't, what is the missing link? I don't really have an easy answer to that. Part of it, though, has to do with the obvious institutional and cultural tendencies to commodify knowledge in informational or economic terms. Poetry *seems* to have little to offer in such a context except to those who intend to teach or write poems. We are, all of us, conditioned by years and years of such tacit messages to read poets without any sense that they may have a more direct connection to our lives. But they can. In this case, the key to getting the full impact of the poem, as I discussed with the class along the way (and will get to in more detail later in the book), is to stand as fully as possible, as if it matters to *us*, in the place that the poet, Coleridge, opens up for us to stand in: the wedding guest's, so mesmerized by the mariner's "glittering eye" that he cannot turn away from the riveting story unfolding before him, despite his desire to do so. This is a mode of reading that can, I believe, lead to an experience, a knowledge, even potentially a wisdom, that is both legitimate and more efficiently achieved than our own actual lifetime allows. This is what I was looking for when I started reading poets, and it is what I'm still looking for. For many of my students this semester that didn't happen. It's fair to ask why I didn't do a better job of teaching there what I'm apparently preaching here. But whether or how this is a directly teachable matter is as arguable as the problem of the teachability of virtue that Socrates comes at repeatedly without ultimate resolution in so many of his dialogues. In any case, I didn't consider this a "failure" either of the poem or of my teaching of it. Universal success is a lot to ask from a first pass at the first poem we read in the course. I thought it worked out pretty well that at least some of the students were moved enough by the poem to feel they gained something of value from it. I suspect they didn't expect such an outcome when they started. And we had a good discussion about this matter of experience and where it comes from, which may help facilitate for some of the other students a more engaged reading of this poem, or another, at some later date.

The one figure I haven't talked about yet is the poet, Coleridge. What is his stake in the wisdom of this poem and how does it affect our reading of it? This is the hardest part of the equation to think about with *this* poem because it is not rendered in "his" voice and is so highly artificial (all those intentionally Gothic trappings) in its rendition. In addition, Coleridge himself, perhaps the first truly great practical critic, had a lot to say, both positive and negative, about this poem. But for all of his very loquacious and extensive writing about himself and his work, Coleridge is a notoriously remote and often unreliable witness. So you can't, or at least I don't, depend on him for an explanation. All I will say about this at the outset is that when I read this poem for the first time and every time I have read it since—dozens of times—Coleridge the author, who concocts the whole thing, is always the ultimate partner to my conversation. Not the elder Coleridge I came to know about later, afflicted and hobbled by his addictions, whose bipolarity is characterized blandly by Thomas Carlyle as "weakness under the possibility of strength" (*LJS* 53), a man who basically could not stop talking and made almost no sense to his listener, but the younger Coleridge, who captures that same bipolarity in such a playfully understated way, in a 1796 letter to John Threlwall, with the phrase "indolence capable of energies," the man who planned to start his utopian Pantisocracy in Pennsylvania, not far from where I grew up. I conjure him as a man who must have had a deep understanding, grounded in his experiences, of psychological suffering, of deprivation, of loneliness, of fear, of guilt and expiation, and, ultimately, of what it means when the mariner "blessed [the water-snakes] unaware" (524, 285) at the moral turning point of his story. I think of him as "goodly company" to "walk together with" (529, 601–2). It is Coleridge, as an active agent in the transaction, who facilitates my entering the position of the wedding guest. That is how he comes to "life" as an author when I read his great poem.

❦

JOHN STUART MILL OFFERS AN EXPLANATION of how poets and poetry differ from "eloquence":

> Poetry and eloquence are both alike the expression or utterance of feeling: but, if we may be excused the antithesis, we should say that eloquence is *heard*; poetry is *over*heard. Eloquence supposes an audience. The peculiarity of poetry appears to us to lie in the poet's utter unconsciousness of a listener. Poetry is feeling confessing itself to itself in moments of solitude . . .
>   All poetry is of the nature of soliloquy. (71)

Of all the poets I've ever read, William Wordsworth best creates this illusion of being "overheard" as he delivers a "soliloquy," which is probably why Mill liked him so much. Yet unlike Mill's description, Wordsworth never seems utterly unconscious of a listener. It's more like he's so fully conscious of a listener that the listener is absorbed *into* the aura of the soliloquy, thereby echoing the experience being rendered, making possible a very special kind of interanimation. His "Ode: Intimations of Immortality from Recollections of Early Childhood" is a good place to start looking at how Wordsworth does this.

In a mixed but astute review of Wordsworth's work, William Hazlitt, one of Wordsworth's contemporaries, calls attention in a negative way to Wordsworth's overwhelming immersion in his own inner world, one so vast and powerful it ends up absorbing all the outside world into it: "He only sympathizes with those simple forms of feeling which mingle at once with his own identity. . . . All accidental varieties and individual contrasts are lost in an endless continuity of feeling; like drops of water in the ocean-stream! An intense intellectual egotism swallows up every thing" (708).

Wordsworth would probably not much dispute most of this. In an explanatory note for his "Ode" he identifies two things as keystones to his own childhood experiences: "Nothing was more difficult for me in childhood than to admit the notion of death as a state applicable to my own being"; and, secondly, "I was often unable to think of external things as having external existence, and communed with all that I saw as something not apart from, but inherent in, my own immaterial nature. Many times while going to school have I grasped at a wall or a tree to recall myself from this abyss of idealism to the reality" (331). In a later letter he claims: "The poem rests entirely upon two recollections of childhood [as noted above]. A Reader who has not a vivid recollection of these feelings having existed in his mind cannot understand that poem" (331).

Fair enough. I certainly shared these two "recollections" with Wordsworth when I first read this poem. So, you might say, I make an ideal reader of his work. But, really, who hasn't as a child at least had the former "notion of death"? And, while the latter sense of the "abyss of idealism" might seem stranger and scarier, as it was to Wordsworth himself by his own admission, he also believed that "every one, if he would look back, could bear testimony" to "that dream-like vividness and splendour which invest objects of sight in childhood" (331). In effect, as he sees it, we're all on the same page in these two respects. So as he voices his own inner soliloquy here about what he has lost, he is speaking not just to, but also about and, ultimately, for us. As the poem progresses, his voice merges with, then becomes indistinguishable from our own.

At least in my first pass through the poem (I'll come back to it in later chapters), I want to focus primarily on the rhetorical techniques Wordsworth uses to achieve this pretty slick and very moving effect. Wordsworth asserts the basic premise of his argument in the first line of the poem's epigraph, "The Child is father of the Man," which he borrows from a short poem, "My Heart Leaps Up When I Behold (330), that he had recently composed. This sense of the primacy of childhood is a fairly standard element of Romantic ideology, hearkening back to Rousseau, for example. But the enigmatic, even cryptic, nature of Wordsworth's expression creates a very pleasant sort of disequilibrium, intriguing enough at the outset to buy enough patience from most readers to draw them into the argument itself.

The opening stanza lays out a very stark then/now pattern to orchestrate the sense of loss that Wordsworth wants to explore in the poem:

> There was a time when meadow, grove and stream,
> The earth, and every common sight,
> To me did seem
> Apparelled in celestial light,
> The glory and the freshness of a dream.
> It is not now as it hath been of yore;—
> Turn wheresoe'er I may
> By night or day,
> The things which I have seen I now can see no more. (331, 1–9)

There is an ease and a poignancy to Wordsworth's nostalgic reverie that is captivating, beckoning us toward our own comparable reverie. One of the ways he accomplishes this, as I will document in various ways throughout the book, is by creating very inviting negative spaces for us to inhabit, absences vast enough to accommodate not just his experiences, which we get to witness through their often quite generic-sounding representations ("meadow, grove and stream," for example), but also and equally importantly our own, which, if we accede to the "dream" Wordsworth promotes, will inevitably draw us into a position to learn what he has to teach.

The second stanza amplifies this then/now disjunction, with an equally harsh and jarring final line to punctuate it:

> The Rainbow comes and goes,
> And lovely is the Rose,
> The Moon doth with delight
> Look round her when the heavens are bare,
> Waters on a starry night
> Are beautiful and fair;
> The sunshine is a glorious birth;
> But yet I know, where'er I go,
> That there hath past away a glory from the earth. (331, 10–18)

All the same natural things are still there and we still see them. But their "glory" has "past away." Wordsworth is framing his problem as a stark binary, for subsequent examination, and it is a common human problem: The past, especially childhood, often looks a lot better than now does. The sense of loss that accompanies this realization tends for most of us most of the time just to depress us. We wait for the feeling to pass, and it recurs in the same form repeatedly. Wordsworth seems to want to talk himself out of this gloomy habit once and for all, and we get to listen in, with, perhaps, some similarly salutary effects.

In the following stanza, the argument begins to turn. Wordsworth fights off his "thought of grief" and reasserts the "now" as the source of his strength:

> Now, while the birds thus sing a joyous song,
> And while the young lambs bound
> As to the tabor's sound,
> To me alone there came a thought of grief:

> A timely utterance gave that thought relief,
>   And I again am strong:
> The cataracts blow their trumpets from the steep;
> No more shall grief of mine the season wrong;
> I hear the Echoes through the mountains throng,
> The Winds come to me from the fields of sleep,
>   And all the earth is gay;
>   Land and sea
>   Give themselves up to jollity,
>   And with the heart of May
>   Doth every Beast keep holiday;—
>   Thou Child of Joy,
> Shout round me, let me hear thy shouts, thou happy
>   Shepherd-boy! (332, 9–35)

These first moves toward restoration sound pretty forced to me, the way such self-persuasions often do at the start: "land and sea give themselves up to jollity," "let me hear thy shouts, thou happy / Shepherd-boy!" I just don't buy it.

In the next stanza, he turns his address outward, bringing not just us but the surrounding landscape of natural things, and even all "the Children . . . culling fresh flowers," into his earshot, as participatory overhearers:

> Ye blessed Creatures, I have heard the call
>   Ye to each other make; I see
> The heavens laugh with you in your jubilee;
>   My heart is at your festival,
>   My head hath its coronal,
> The fulness of your bliss, I feel—I feel it all.
>   Oh evil day! if I were sullen
>   While Earth herself is adorning,
>   This sweet May-morning,
>   And the Children are culling
>   On every side,
>   In a thousand valleys far and wide,
>   Fresh flowers; while the sun shines warm,
> And the Babe leaps up on his Mother's arm:—
>   I hear, I hear, with joy I hear!
>   —But there's a Tree, of many, one,

A single Field which I have looked upon,
Both of them speak of something that is gone:
      The Pansy at my feet
      Doth the same tale repeat:
Whither is fled the visionary gleam?
Where is it now, the glory and the dream?

Again, this is a pretty standard mode of self-persuasion. And it doesn't take entirely, as is clear when he sees "a Tree, of many, one" and is back down in the dumps again. But there seems finally to be some traction for Wordsworth's ascent.

The next four stanzas narrate a more reasoned argument for believing that not only is death not the end of life, but also that there is a life *before* this one, from which we come, "trailing clouds of glory." The structure of this part of the argument can be indexed by the opening lines of each stanza. The first two sound like teacherly explanations:

Our birth is but a sleep and a forgetting:
The Soul that rises with us, our life's Star,
      Hath had elsewhere its setting,
        And cometh from afar:
      Not in entire forgetfulness,
      And not in utter nakedness,
But trailing clouds of glory do we come
      From God, who is our home:
Heaven lies about us in our infancy!
Shades of the prison-house begin to close
      Upon the growing Boy,
But He beholds the light, and whence it flows,
      He sees it in his joy;
The Youth, who daily farther from the east
      Must travel, still is Nature's Priest,
      And by the vision splendid
      Is on his way attended;
At length the Man perceives it die away,
And fade into the light of common day.

Earth fills her lap with pleasures of her own;
Yearnings she hath in her own natural kind,

> And, even with something of a Mother's mind,
>> And no unworthy aim,
>> The homely Nurse doth all she can
> To make her Foster-child, her Inmate Man,
>> Forget the glories he hath known,
> And that imperial palace whence he came. (332, 58–84)

Wordsworth's argument for the child being father of the man is roughly Platonic, along the lines that Socrates lays out in the *Meno* and the *Phaedo*. For Socrates, the knowledge we acquired in previous lives is forgotten, by dint of our human condition, at birth, and we must then work to recollect as much of it as we can through learning and reflection. Wordsworth focuses instead, as is often his habit, on what we forget gradually, almost grudgingly, on our progress through this life. Though Wordsworth later wrote a long disclaimer about his actual "faith" in such a non-Christian notion of immortality (he said he just wanted to "make the best use of it I could as a Poet"), the sense of deathlessness that he felt as a child and wants so much to recover, now has a "sufficient foundation," an adult argument to support it (331).

Stanza VII then asks us, from the outside, to "Behold the Child among his new-born blisses," thus, finally, engaging us directly in the movement of the poem. And by stanza VIII, Wordsworth addresses the child directly: "Thou, whose exterior semblance doth belie / Thy Soul's immensity." Because Wordsworth has already hooked us rhetorically, we instinctively feel that we, too, are addressing the child, a very emotion-laden position from which to contemplate the question at hand. It is as if his soliloquy has become a kind of ventriloquy, his words becoming ours becoming his:

> Behold the Child among his new-born blisses,
> A six years' Darling of a pigmy size!
> See, where 'mid work of his own hand he lies,
> Fretted by sallies of his mother's kisses,
> With light upon him from his father's eyes!
> See, at his feet, some little plan or chart,
> Some fragment from his dream of human life,
> Shaped by himself with newly-learned art;
>> A wedding or a festival,
>> A mourning or a funeral;
>>> And this hath now his heart,
>> And unto this he frames his song:

Then will he fit his tongue
To dialogues of business, love, or strife;
But it will not be long
Ere this be thrown aside,
And with new joy and pride
The little Actor cons another part;
Filling from time to time his "humorous stage"
With all the Persons, down to palsied Age,
That Life brings with her in her equipage;
As if his whole vocation
Were endless imitation.

Thou, whose exterior semblance doth belie
Thy Soul's immensity;
Thou best Philosopher, who yet dost keep
Thy heritage, thou Eye among the blind,
That, deaf and silent, read'st the eternal deep,
Haunted for ever by the eternal mind,—
Mighty Prophet! Seer blest!
On whom those truths do rest,
Which we are toiling all our lives to find,
In darkness lost, the darkness of the grave;
Thou, over whom thy Immortality
Broods like the Day, a Master o'er a Slave,
A Presence which is not to be put by;
Thou little Child, yet glorious in the might
Of heaven-born freedom on thy being's height,
Why with such earnest pains dost thou provoke
The years to bring the inevitable yoke,
Thus blindly with thy blessedness at strife?
Full soon thy Soul shall have her earthly freight,
And custom lie upon thee with a weight
Heavy as frost, and deep almost as life! (332–33, 85–128)

The final three stanzas—opening with the exclamation "O joy!"—have such a resolute, Beethovian clarity to them, an innocence even, but of the adult and not the childish kind. Yes, a lot has been lost in the migration out of those clouds of glory and into "the inevitable yoke" of our "earthly freight." But what remains, he insists, is great beyond measure:

O joy! that in our embers
Is something that doth live,
That nature yet remembers
What was so fugitive!
The thought of our past years in me doth breed
Perpetual benediction: not indeed
For that which is most worthy to be blest—
Delight and liberty, the simple creed
Of Childhood, whether busy or at rest,
With new-fledged hope still fluttering in his breast:—
Not for these I raise
The song of thanks and praise;
But for those obstinate questionings
Of sense and outward things,
Fallings from us, vanishings;
Blank misgivings of a Creature
Moving about in worlds not realised,
High instincts before which our mortal Nature
Did tremble like a guilty Thing surprised:
But for those first affections,
Those shadowy recollections,
Which, be they what they may,
Are yet the fountain light of all our day,
Are yet a master light of all our seeing;
Uphold us, cherish, and have power to make
Our noisy years seem moments in the being
Of the eternal Silence: truths that wake,
To perish never;
Which neither listlessness, nor mad endeavour,
Nor Man nor Boy,
Nor all that is at enmity with joy,
Can utterly abolish or destroy!
Hence in a season of calm weather
Though inland far we be,
Our Souls have sight of that immortal sea
Which brought us hither,
Can in a moment travel thither,
And see the Children sport upon the shore,
And hear the mighty waters rolling evermore. (333, 129–67)

Wordsworth's peace of mind is palpable at this point, as is ours if we get absorbed enough in his, and the poem coasts gracefully to conclusion. He turns first to address the birds and their joyous song, which he mentioned earlier in the poem, when, as I said, he seemed to be straining. Here everything is clear, calm and deep:

> Then sing, ye Birds, sing, sing a joyous song!
> And let the young Lambs bound
> As to the tabor's sound!
> We in thought will join your throng,
> Ye that pipe and ye that play,
> Ye that through your hearts to-day
> Feel the gladness of the May!
> What though the radiance which was once so bright
> Be now for ever taken from my sight,
> Though nothing can bring back the hour
> Of splendour in the grass, of glory in the flower;
> We will grieve not, rather find
> Strength in what remains behind;
> In the primal sympathy
> Which having been must ever be;
> In the soothing thoughts that spring
> Out of human suffering;
> In the faith that looks through death,
> In years that bring the philosophic mind. (333, 168–86)

Death now overtaken, he can focus on "the dream-like vividness" of *adult* sight, which the closing stanza embodies so well:

> And O, ye Fountains, Meadows, Hills, and Groves,
> Forebode not any severing of our loves!
> Yet in my heart of hearts I feel your might;
> I only have relinquished one delight
> To live beneath your more habitual sway.
> I love the Brooks which down their channels fret,
> Even more than when I tripped lightly as they;
> The innocent brightness of a new-born Day
> Is lovely yet;
> The Clouds that gather round the setting sun

> Do take a sober colouring from an eye
> That hath kept watch o'er man's mortality;
> Another race hath been, and other palms are won.
> Thanks to the human heart by which we live,
> Thanks to its tenderness, its joys, and fears,
> To me the meanest flower that blows can give
> Thoughts that do often lie too deep for tears. (333–34, 187–203)

There are all kinds of strange conversations going on in this poem: Wordsworth talking to himself, to the "blessed Creatures," to the "little Child," to the birds, to the "Fountains, Meadows, Hills and Groves." And there are all kinds of unusual responses that the poet is listening to: The birds' songs, the "tabor's sound," the cataracts, the Shepherd-boy, the "Babe . . . on his Mother's arm," and on and on. Never does Wordsworth try to teach us directly, didactically. His concern is with himself, his personal problem with human mortality. But that problem is universal; we all experience some angst about it. By "overhearing" what goes on in this poem, by bearing witness thereby to Wordsworth's self-persuasion, fully conscious as he is that we are lending an ear, fully confident as he is that he is worth such attention, we stand to gain some knowledge of consequence, in this case without having to go out and initiate all of those potentially awkward conversations on our own.

ANOTHER WAY TO GET AT THIS GENERAL question of what kind of experience a poet proffers is through the nature/books binary, a favorite trope among both the British and American Romantics. The former term in that equation (nature) isn't one that my students usually turn to as their counter to book-learning, probably because we tend to think of that term quite narrowly, in "environmental" terms. Nature for Wordsworth and the American Transcendentalists was so much more than this, not merely the external scenery of the hills and dales, though the wild and rustic were surely a part of what they had in mind. It also named the organic, spiritually infused relationship between mind and world; Wordsworth voices this when he speaks of a "presence . . . a sense sublime . . . a motion and a spirit . . . that . . . rolls through all things" (302, 95–102).

At the opposite pole from nature are books—dead, lifeless things afflicted by the pallor of their pastness. You can see a good example of the nature/books argument in Wordsworth's "Expostulation and Reply" and

"The Tables Turned," the two companion poems in the middle of *Lyrical Ballads,* in which "William," the dreamer, and "Matthew," the practical one, go back and forth in various ways. In the first poem they contend over the relative merits of "books . . . that light bequeath'd / . . . From dead men to their kind" compared to "dream[ing] your time away / . . . In a wise passiveness" (103). In the latter poem, the counterargument is presented straightforwardly in one speaking voice. It opens with a mild rebuke of books as just a lot of "toil and trouble." Then they are "endless strife" (104). Finally, they are the primary suspects supporting Wordsworth's famous critique of "[o]ur meddling intellect," which "Mis-shapes the beauteous forms of things: / We murder to dissect" (105). The alternative to all this malformation at the hands of deadly books is, in these poems at least, to "[l]et Nature be your teacher" (104). That Wordsworth makes his case against books in a book, as did many of his like-minded contemporaries, is a contradiction that remains oddly and provocatively unacknowledged.

Basically, in the road-to-Larissa system, Wordsworth warns us away from the first kind of guide. But what is the alternative? One must first spend some time "dreaming" to get one's own bearings in the world, simply listening to "mother earth" speaking and then learning to converse with her. This is what William's "wise passiveness" is all about. As opposed to dumb passiveness, I suppose, which sees and hears not much of anything from either nature *or* books; or a wise aggressiveness, which strives for certain kinds of accumulation, solutions, destinations, in both arenas. No one though can possibly "learn" everything they need to know simply by sitting forever on a stone and dreaming in "wise passiveness." If you want to write, to think, to engage with culture and tradition in any meaningful way, you must read. Even to know these two poems, which appear to denigrate reading, one must read them. Wordsworth is smart enough to know that. And so are we. So to me, the second type of guide is on the scene here in the subterranean guise of Wordsworth, who guides us indirectly, more by what he leaves out than what he gets in (which is a pretty typical strategy of his) as the poet on the other side of this relationship.

About forty years later, Ralph Waldo Emerson provides a more dramatic take on the nature/book binary in "The American Scholar," where among the "influences" on the developing scholarly mind he ranks nature "first in time and first in importance." Besides the obvious physical aspects of nature—"the sun," "night and her stars," "the wind," "the grass"—Emerson also includes "men and women, conversing, beholding and beholden." In other words, on the surface, Emerson's nature seems to be kind of like the firsthand experience that my students wrote about—roughly, what we bear witness to by observing and listening and interacting with the world in its physical and social aspects. But in "engaging this spectacle" to "settle its value in his mind," the budding scholar moves to a deeper level of scrutiny, by means of which: "He shall see that nature is the opposite of his soul, answering to it part for part. One is seal, and one is print. Its beauty is the beauty of his own mind. Its laws are the laws of his own mind. . . . And, in fine, the ancient, 'Know thyself,' and the modern precept, 'Study nature,' become at last one maxim" (228). Books, on the other hand, the "mind of the Past," are not all bad, in "theory" at least. They are the "truth," "immortal thoughts," and "poetry," of scholarly enterprise, some pretty good things. But they are not "quite perfect" either, afflicted as they inevitably are by "the conventional, the local, the perishable." As long as "each age" recognizes that in-built deficiency of these textual hand-me-downs and writes "its own books," things are fine. Then the argument takes a sharp, negative turn: "Yet hence arises a grave mischief. The sacredness which attaches to the act of creation . . . is transferred to the record . . . [H]enceforth it is settled, the book is perfect. . . . Instantly the book becomes noxious: the guide a tyrant" (229). The leap from not "quite perfect" to "noxious" tyranny is a huge one and it happens just like that. Emerson seems to surpass even Socrates in his suspicion of textual authority. A tyrant, I suppose, could do a very efficient job of taking you to Larissa, but it wouldn't be a very enjoyable trip, even for the most lazy or submissive of travelers. What Emerson calls attention to here, this tyranny, is to me the opposite face of what I call commemoration, which, as Martin Heidegger reminds us, is so often "found side by side" with "thoughtlessness," especially in "memorial celebration[s]" of masterworks (*DT* 44). If you make too much of a book, you make too little of it. And, ultimately, of yourself. So unless you find a way to keep books in their proper place and perspective—more like the second kind of guide Socrates describes—you will, as Emerson says, "look backward and not forward" (230); again, not the best strategy for the traveler who wants to go toward someplace and not just away from where he is.

Emerson proceeds to make a devastating critique of the various ways in which the valorization of books is institutionalized culturally and historically with all manner of deleterious effects. How do we avoid this kind of intellectual desiccation? The scholar does it by "thinking." Emerson's Man Thinking seems like it might offer a third alternative for getting to Larissa: just relying on your own good judgment—properly schooled, in this case, by a prior investment in studying (with the necessary cautions) nature and books—to get you where *you* want to go. Or maybe, more accurately in Emerson's terms, to realize finally that your proper destination is right where you are, "on that plot of ground which is given to [you] to till" (267), which is where the truly great books are written and where they must be read.

This is an initiative that Whitman borrows from Emerson and runs with, sort of like Emerson on speed. Whitman is not just interested in having us listen patiently to a morally instructive story, as Coleridge is, or even having us listen in on, and join, the poet's internal soliloquy, as Wordsworth is. He wants us, cajoles us, commands us, to abandon our customary readerly conventions and manners in quite a radical way so that he might come into a deep partnership, even a fusion, with his reader, as he makes evident in the opening lines from "Song of Myself":

> I celebrate myself
> and what I assume you shall assume.
> For every atom belonging to me belongs as well to you. (28, 1–3)

What could be swifter and more extreme in suggesting not just commonality between poet and reader, but interanimation, transubstantiation even? It takes Whitman a mere three lines to move from what appears at first to be a simple, expressive, autobiographical "I" to a fully animated "you," the reader as engaged interlocutor, who is invited into an open, epic realm shared equally, down to the atomic level, by both the parties.

Whitman goes way beyond Wordsworth, who simply entices us into his inner world, wherein our voices, should we share the concerns of the specific poem we are reading, are gradually modulated into his. Wordsworth's process is relatively invisible and tacit. And when the poem is done, the experience is over. Whitman strives throughout "Song of Myself" to break down the seemingly insuperable cultural and historical barriers—and even the customary psychic boundaries—between himself and others, first, and then between himself and us, his readers. His "every atom belonging to me belongs as well to you" seems, as the poem opens, like a vague metaphor for the sort of "we are all of stardust made" clichés we bandy about in our TV-level philosophical moods. But as the poem goes on, it becomes clear he has the real thing in mind here. All the extensive catalogues of things natural, of people, their stories, his merger over and over with everything he sees, touches, smells, his periodic wrangling with us, directly, as parties to this process, it's all very exhausting. I've never, to be honest, been able to read through the whole of "Song of Myself" without stopping for a while to come back to *my* self. I've had no such problem with Wordsworth or Coleridge. Whitman seems always to be in overdrive, on the almost much-too-much side, at least for my nervous system. I'm afraid at times that I might end up going too far to come back.

There is one point in the poem where Whitman has that same fear himself, where he seems to get exhausted and confused in much the same way as I do. And it offers an opportunity to get at some sense of just how much he's trying to teach us through this poem. It's in (what became in later editions) section 38 of the poem, where he addresses us directly (in French) as students:

> Eleves I salute you,
> I see the approach of your numberless gangs . . . . I see you
>   understand yourselves and me,
> And know that they who have eyes are divine, and the blind and
>   lame are equally divine . . . (78, 968–70)

Right before this "salute" to us, in one of the most cryptic sections of the poem, after a pages-and-pages-long series of personal transfigurations—"I am a free companion" (69, 813), "I am the hounded slave" (70, 833), "I am an old artillerist" (71, 853), etc., etc.—and several much longer and very sorrowful stories about the horrors of war (72–76, sections 34–36), told as if from the inside, Whitman seems to have reached a state of such ecstatic empathy, such a nearly complete breakdown of his own personal identity—"O Christ! My fit is mastering me!" (76, 933)—that he begins to identify with all the world's sufferers almost simultaneously. But then he catches himself:

> Somehow I have been stunned. Stand back!
> Give me a little time beyond my cuffed head and slumbers and
>   dreams and gaping,
> I discover myself on a verge of the usual mistake.
>
> That I could forget the mockers and insults!
> That I could forget the trickling tears and the blows of the bludgeons
>   and hammers!
> That I could look with a separate look on my own crucifixion and
>   bloody crowning!
>
> I remember . . . I resume the overstayed fraction . . . (77, 955–60)

What is he talking about here? Clearly there is some sort of Christ-like suffering, death, and resurrection that he imagines himself enduring. But what did he forget and what does he now remember to take him into the final fourth of the poem, the discourse of which is much more disjointed, casual, self-conscious, fragmentary, even at times playfully humorous? No longer is he lost in his empathic transfigurations into all those sufferers suffering. He remembers the "mockers" and their "insults," and understands that they, too, play a human role in the dramas at hand. And he remembers himself, as someone who suffers all this in his own right, as an individual identity he cannot simply objectify from the outside with "a separate look." He knows he is just "one of an average unending procession"—and we are there with him—"We walk the roads . . ."—all of us, on our way "over the whole earth" (77–78, 962–66). This is Whitman the mystic coming out of his long learning period to assume, finally, the position of Whitman the teacher, but in a very peculiar way: "Behold I do not give lectures or a little charity. / What I give I give out of myself" (79, 990–91). It certainly seems like a quixotic, ambitious, exorbitant pedagogical position, by academic standards, at least. And it asks that we assume a comparably quixotic, ambitious, and exorbitant position as his pupils, his "eleves"—"I do not ask who you are . . . that is not important to me. / You can do nothing and be nothing but what I will infold in you" (79, 996–97). But go along with it we must if we want to join him on his journey. And it is, to me at least, a very ethereal, exhilarating, and joyous ride from here to the poem's end.

This merger down to the atomic level somehow leaves us, oddly enough, free to fulfill the seemingly (at the time) unrealistic promise Whitman makes early in the poem:

> Have you reckoned a thousand acres much? Have you reckoned the
> earth much?
> Have you practiced so long to learn to read?
> Have you felt so proud to get at the meaning of poems?
>
> Stop this day and night with me and you shall possess the origin of all
> poems,
> You shall possess the good of the earth and sun . . . there are millions
> of suns left,
> You shall no longer take things at second or third hand . . . nor look
> through the eyes of the dead . . . nor feed on the spectres in books,

> You shall not look through my eyes either, nor take things from me,
> You shall listen to all sides and filter them from yourself. (29, 23–28)

Whitman exiles the traditional mode of reading; this poem has no meaning in that particular way. If we "stop this day" with him we "shall possess the origins of all poems," by which I take him to mean we will become poets of a sort in our own right. Paradoxically, in the process, we will come to "possess" nature in a conception more radical than that of either his mentor Emerson or his predecessor Wordsworth, in that it is induced expressly by the "book" that is being rendered and read. The claim that we "shall not look through [his] eyes either" I can accept only in a very mixed way. Clearly, by subverting and multiplying the unitary, monolithic "I" of traditional lyric poetry, he also subverts and multiplies the "eye" that is its most static and local instrument. This is something more than Emerson's "transparent eyeball"—"I am nothing. I see all" (184)—and it is something more than the "wise passiveness" we encounter through Wordsworth's William.

What Whitman has to offer is also, to be sure, a few big notches above what I was trying to think about as a teenager, as I'll detail in my history of reading this poem later in the book. But it is the most accurate representation of the conundrum that I started with, both forty-some years ago and in this argument. The key is not in the type of poem being proffered, though "Song of Myself" insists on the mode of reading I am trying to elucidate. The key is in our manner of engaging with the poet who proffers it. Any poet lends himself to being engaged in such a way that his poem approximates, without ever fully infringing upon, our own experience.

The gist of Whitman's invitation is that in the process of reading his poem, the reader will transcend the process of reading and begin a process of writing. Or, perhaps, that for a poem of a particular sort, the kind that Whitman is writing—one that abrogates in every conceivable way the traditional authoritative locus of both of the authorial, lyric "I" and the readerly, essentialized "I"—the act of reading is already, in itself, a mode of composition, one that culminates neither in understanding the poem (in the mode of close reading) nor in re-writing the poem in the reading (in the mode of reader-response or deconstruction), but in going off to write a book of one's own. Not one modeled on Whitman's but one inspired by it. Whitman is not simply offering himself as a right-minded guide who can get us to Larissa by *either* of the means Socrates proffers. He tells us to trust our own judgment and take the trip ourselves by another method. And if we do, guaranteed, we will find a Larissa different from his, and call it something else.

✤

IT'S ONE THING, YOU MIGHT SAY, to read poets in this way when they invite such a relationship by declaring so openly their sense of commonalty and equality with their prospective audience, as Wordsworth and Whitman do. But what about poets who don't? T. S. Eliot is part of the "intellectual drift of moment" I refer to earlier in relation to Richards's project. Eliot's famously seminal book of essays *The Sacred Wood* preceded Richards's book by about a decade. In it, he writes:

> It is not in his personal emotions, the emotions provoked by particular events in his life, that the poet is in any way remarkable or interesting. . . . The business of the poet is not to find new emotions, but to use the ordinary ones and, in working them up into poetry, to express feelings which are not in actual emotions at all. And emotions which he has never experienced will serve his turn as well as those familiar to him. Consequently, we must believe that "emotion recollected in tranquillity" is an inexact formula. For it is neither emotion, nor recollection, nor, without distortion of meaning, tranquillity. . . . There is a great deal, in the writing of poetry, which must be conscious and deliberate. In fact, the bad poet is usually unconscious where he ought to be conscious, and conscious where he ought to be unconscious. Both errors tend to make him "personal." Poetry is not a turning loose of emotion, but an escape from emotion; it is not the expression of personality, but an escape from personality. But, of course, only those who have personality and emotions know what it means to want to escape from these things. (*SW* 58)

Eliot is not one to recommend taking his name off the poem before anyone reads it. He doesn't have to. There is not much risk of getting too enamored of a poet who has worked so hard to avoid the two greatest "errors" that might "tend to make him 'personal.'" Even a poet like Eliot, though—who quite expressly seeks to depersonalize the position of the poet in order to differentiate him from a "common" audience; and who then uses a variety of formal gestures in a poem like "The Waste Land" to enforce this differentiation—can be understood in some fundamental way, if one takes a direct and collegial approach.

I read "The Waste Land" for the first time in my sophomore year of college, during the second term of a year-long introduction to English literature course, for which we used the *Norton Anthology of English Literature*, the gold standard of anthologies at the time. My teacher for both terms was a man who had been blind for most of his life, who read everything in Braille, a large, imposing African American man with a reputation (well earned and deserved) for being brilliant, demanding, and difficult. Many myths circulated about his amazing powers—that he could walk around campus without a seeing-eye dog or cane by whistling and hearing the echoes—and especially about his ill-tempered stringency in the classroom. I was very apprehensive when I found out I was going to have him for this, my first college English course. I vowed to myself to keep my head down and avoid his attentions, at least until I got my feet on the ground.

Our first assignment was to read the first section of volume 1 of the *Norton*, which was on "the epic." I can't remember everything that entailed, but it included a list of the typical features of Western epic poems, which I memorized. At the start of the next class, first thing, he ran his hand down the Braille enrollment list and stopped: "Mr. KAM-een (he overemphasized the first syllable, I remember, putting me on edge), give me an epic." I panicked. I was quite sure a teacher that demanding, wanting to establish his regime early, would not be using his first question to get me just to *name* one (which was, in fact, all he wanted). I wanted to list for him the features of the epic I had memorized, but the question clearly didn't call for that. What could he possibly want from me? So I decided to ask, and my question came back this way: "Do you want me just to name an epic or come up with one?" As soon as I heard what I had actually said I knew I was screwed in a way I could never explain myself out of. Not just right then but forever, with him. A barely audible collective gasp rose up from the rest of the class, which could not believe my apparent flippancy, and because I had, in effect, poked the tiger, endangering everyone. He took this as a direct affront to his authority—understandably so, if I had meant to say it that way, which of course I didn't. We did not get along well after that, ever.

Late in that year (I drew him for my second term as well), having plugged away in my doghouse for six or seven months by then (I had worked my grade up into the B+ range and I was feeling more confident and comfortable in the class), we came to "The Waste Land." My only previous exposure to Eliot was with "The Hollow Men" which, oddly, in my sophomore year in high school, our class had to memorize in order to do a choral reading, open to the public, in the school gym. I had forgotten all about this until right now. I can't imagine how any teacher would consider a performance of that poem, rendered through thirty or so teenage voices, appealing small-town entertainment. The audience was primarily our parents and relatives, deeply religious, hard-working, up-by-the-bootstraps people. Eliot's despairing vision would be anathema to them. And besides, who wants to hear their sons and daughters claim with severity, if not pride, to be hollow and filled with straw? But that's what we did, for all who came to endure it. I knew from this experience that Eliot was considered deep and difficult, kind of beyond the range of someone my age, though "The Hollow Men" seemed straightforward enough. These are the opening lines, as I remember having delivered them in my part of the chorus:

> We are the hollow men
> We are the stuffed men
> Leaning together
> Headpiece filled with straw. Alas! (*Poems* 123)

What's so hard to get about that? I thought at the time that the real mystery of Eliot, the great guru of twentieth-century poetry, must be locked up somewhere else, like in "The Waste Land." So when we got to it in the course, I felt a great sense of anticipation, like now, finally, I was going to get the keys to the kingdom. I wanted to get going.

I read through the poem thinking, yes, it's difficult in certain ways, dense, formally disjunctive, but not too bad. You have the haughty, blathering German lady, nostalgic, boring, with upper-class affectations, through whom Eliot ventriloquizes the poem's opening ("I read, much of the night, and go south in the winter" [*WL*, line 18]). The vampy Madame Sosostris who reads the tarot cards ("Fear death by water" [55]). The ditzy ladies in the bar at the bartender's last call ("Goodnight ladies, good night" [172]). Hermaphroditic, voyeuristic Tiresius foretelling the bored, tired typist's evening under the groping hands of the "young man carbuncular" ("Well now that's done: and I'm glad it's over" [252]). Creepy Phlebus the Phoenecian dead in the sea ("Consider Phlebus, who was once handsome and tall as you" [321]). Prajapi from the Upanishads delivering the triple whammy at the end. All these ghostly disembodied forms, these talking heads knocking around the echo-chamber of modern culture like raccoons in a garbage can: "I had not thought death had undone so many" (63). I liked it and I thought I got it pretty well.

Then I turned to the footnotes and my jaw dropped. I had never seen a poem with footnotes provided by the author, and the first few are doozies, implying a need to read all of Jessie L. Westin's *From Ritual to Romance* and

James George Frazer's multivolume *The Golden Bough* just to understand the *context* for the poem. Part of me thought, God, I have to read all of these books just to get a sense of what's going on here? That's impressive. I'd better get going. English is a very deep field. And part of me just wanted to laugh: Who does Eliot think he's kidding? I pictured him as a pipe-smoking, effete-sounding, professorial type saying: "Yes, young man, you must get started; perhaps someday you will understand what you must to be able read this poem; then come and talk to me." The impressed part of me felt a pride to see verified in this way my underlying sense that poetry was in fact a deeply intellectual enterprise. The skeptical part wondered whether this was just an authorial tour de force, a scam really, meant to demean me into an attitude of subservience toward *his* deeply intellectual enterprise. This schizoid split in my response to the poem has remained in place, largely in this same form, ever since. I can't decide whether to buckle down to do more work or just laugh and ignore the puffery. So, when I read Eliot, I end up doing both in some unpredictable combination. Not resolving this dilemma has, over the long run, become the keystone to what has been my enduring and productive relationship with Eliot. And that is the point I want to make about this process of re-reading: we don't ever need simply to accede in a simplistic, robotic way to tacit ambitions that a poet has for us as readers, and we needn't insist that the poet accede to ours. We don't even have to get along that well with one another. I spend lots of time profitably around people I don't get along with very well, including my teacher when I first read this poem as a college sophomore.

Every poet seeks to position his or readers in certain ways, often by asserting authority. That is part of the prerogative of an author's "life," just as it is for any other living person we encounter. But as readers (and colleagues and friends and spouses) we are equally authorized to stake a claim of our own. And we should be doing so, by which means we acknowledge and affirm both our own life *and* the author's. Here there is a possibility for equipoise, for collaborative tension, for a clear you and a clear me who are equally "alive" at the moment; in other words, a real relationship. That's how all relationships work and grow. I may not always, or ever really, get along very well with Eliot. But I do have a relationship with him and I enjoy re-reading his great poem.

♣

WHEN YOU START TO READ POETS such that they begin to inflect, amplify, and supplement your "personal" experience in deep and significant ways, you begin also to take an interest in matters of method, form, approach, perspective—not necessarily so you can write similar poems of your own, and not simply to re-experience what the poet thought and felt. You do it to have a new experience of your own, preferably one that you didn't come pre-wired for. Let me offer some examples of what I mean by this. I'll begin with an argument that T. S Eliot and William Carlos Williams had in the early stages of the modernist movement.

Both Eliot and Williams were opening their careers during World War I, under the sponsorship of Ezra Pound, the Godfather of most of the early modernists. Both knew that the cultural and ideological foundation supporting the poetics that dominated the nineteenth century were being destabilized by the war and both were searching for something different to replace them. Williams was a doctor from Paterson, New Jersey, in search of what he called the "American idiom," a poetic, in Whitman's spirit, expressly outside the shadow of European traditions. Eliot, on the other hand, emigrated to England in 1914 and immersed himself in what he called "the mind of Europe" (*SW* 102), particularly French symbolist poetry of the late nineteenth century. Around this time they were both still under the general sway of the imagist movement that Pound helped to found and promulgate in England. Among the three tenets of imagism, as first listed in an article titled "Imagisme" that the group published in the March 1913 issue of *Poetry* (under F. S. Flint's name, but with Pound's fingerprints all over it) this was the first: "Direct treatment of the 'thing,' whether subjective or objective" (95; see also Pound, "A Few Don'ts").

All poetry, all discourse I suppose, depends on some set of assumptions about the relationship, or lack of one, between subjective and objective "things," between inside and outside. For the Romantics, this was generally unproblematic. Wordsworth is a good example. When he talks about poetry arising from "emotion recollected in tranquillity" (432) the emotion is clearly and simply his, entirely on the inside; and it was generally engendered by some prior contact with nature, the equally stable outside. For the modernists, such a confident Cartesian binary just wasn't there anymore; they had to find new ways to orchestrate this relationship.

Many of the arguments among twentieth-century poets have been about which one of these two categories of "things" should hold primacy in a poem, in other words whether poems should work from the inside out or from the outside in. Consider the following passages, the first by Eliot, the second by Williams:

April is the cruelest month, breeding
Lilacs out of the dead land, mixing
Memory and desire, stirring
Dull roots with spring rain. (*WL,* lines 1–4)

Black eyed susan
Rich orange
Round the purple core (*Im* 151)

It is quite clear even on a first read that Eliot asks us to stand in a different relationship to his lilacs than Williams does to his black-eyed susan. Eliot's lilacs are "things," but they are not being presented to us here primarily as and for themselves. Instead, they carry one of the many "feelings" that constitute the pastiche of "The Waste Land." In other words, they are *subjective* things. Once we understand that—and it's pretty hard not to, given how he characterizes the lilacs—Eliot's method in the poem becomes evident. As we read on, we understand that the women in the pub, the "young man carbuncular" and his date, Madame Sosostris, all of them are poetic inventions arranged in sequence to achieve certain intellectual and emotional effects. It may take several readings, even some research, to fully grasp the multi-layered quality of the lilacs—like their allusive relationship with Whitman's elegy for Lincoln, "When Lilacs Last in the Dooryard Bloomed," which brings its own feelings into the poem as nuances, even though it is literally absent. But that is a natural direction for his method to take.

Williams's black eyed susan on the other hand is clearly a real flower in its own right, which we are called on to *see* in order to enter into the imaginative world it engenders. The poem goes on to riff through a couple of "things" that are *not* there with the black eyed susan: white daisies, farmers who live poorly. But even these have an objective cast to them, taking us deeper into the reality that the black eyed susan opens up. Finally, he addresses the flower directly:

But you
are rich
in savagery—

Arab
Indian
dark woman (151)

The leap he makes at the end here, to the various kinds of exotics the flower helps him to conjure, is like the one I'll talk about in more detail below. The point I want to make now is that Williams's method tends to begin with a real perception of an actual thing, which he then transmutes imaginatively through the poem.

We can find ample evidence to support all of this, and to understand the sharp disagreement between the two, in the poets' critical writing. Eliot, for example, wrote his dissertation on F. H. Bradley, a British idealist philosopher, who reflected Eliot's own skepticism about human communication. One avenue into the difficulties this philosophical predilection creates for a poet is Eliot's concept of "emotion," a term that comes up over and over again in his essay "Tradition and the Individual Talent." Eliot's emotions are quite a bit different from Wordsworth's, and he spends half a page critiquing Wordsworth's position, quoting directly from Wordsworth's "Preface" to the *Lyrical Ballads*, without ever mentioning Wordsworth's name.

Eliot's distinction between emotions and feelings is an important one for Bradley, for whom feelings are the conceptual equivalent of ideas in traditional idealist philosophy. But I'm more interested here in the practical problem that a position like this presents when a poet, with all those emotions floating in the closed sphere of his experience, has something he wants to get across to his readers. How is that possible? Eliot solves this problem with his concept of the "objective correlative:" "The only way of expressing emotion in the form of art is by finding an 'objective correlative'; in other words, a set of objects, a situation, a chain of events which shall be the formula of that *particular* emotion; such that when the external facts, which must terminate in sensory experience, are given, the emotion is immediately evoked" (100). The poem, then, is a kind of puzzle assembled by the poet from the various inner bits and pieces required to stand for its motive "emotion." These things—objects, situations, chains of events—are not being rendered on their own terms. They are part of a precisely regulated poetic calculus. All of this comes from "[t]he poet's mind [which] is in fact a receptacle for seizing and storing up numberless feelings, phrases, images, which remain there until all the particles which can unite to form a new compound are present together" (55).

That is the basic law of gravity that governs the workings of an Eliot poem. "The Waste Land" is the epitome of this method. And it is why, when Eliot published it in 1922, Williams was devastated by this "great catastrophe to our letters" (*Au* 146). He felt that the new poetic he championed was now doomed, and another version of the old poetic would triumph. As he further laments:

> Then out of the blue the *Dial* brought out *The Waste Land* and all our hilarity ended. It wiped out our world as if an atom bomb had been dropped upon it and our brave sallies into the unknown were turned to dust.
>
> To me especially it struck like a sardonic bullet. I felt at once that it had set me back twenty years, and I'm sure it did. Critically Eliot returned us to the classroom just at the moment when I felt that we were on the point of an escape to matters much closer to the essence of a new art form itself—rooted in the locality which should give it fruit. I knew at once that in certain ways I was most defeated.
>
> Eliot had turned his back on the possibility of reviving my world. And being an accomplished craftsman, better skilled in some ways than I could ever hope to be, I had to watch him carry my world off with him, the fool, to the enemy. (*Au* 174)

What, we might fairly ask, could be at stake here that warrants such a dire discourse? Williams provides the answer to all of this, as well as a partial rebuttal to Eliot's agenda, in his raucous *Spring and All* published in 1923. Williams's spring is quite a bit different from Eliot's April, and this book is a masterful, messy mélange of prose passages (many obviously ironic or sarcastic, some nonsensical), intentional errors (misnumbered pages, upside-down titles), and an assortment of precise, highly disciplined, beautiful little poems, all without any footnotes or allusions. Even those random strands of New Jersey landscape that crop up in the poems that might seem like waste lands—"the road to the contagious hospital," for example—are only "[l]ifeless in appearance" as "spring approaches"; "rooted they / grip down and begin to awaken" (*Im* 95–96).

Williams is not simply offering "nature" as a counter to Eliot's "books." For him, the poem creates "new form dealt with as reality in itself" (133). It is the imagination that forges this reality by a very specific process: "Imagination is not to avoid reality, nor is it description nor an evocation of objects or situations [notice the sly reference to Eliot's definition of the objective correlative], it is to say that poetry does not tamper with the world but moves it—It affirms reality most powerfully and therefore . . . it creates a new object, a play, a dance which is not a mirror up to nature but—" (149–50). Williams stops this sentence short of its resolution, as he does so often in *Spring and All,* creating both tension and an open space for our speculations; but his next paragraph offers an analogy to help us toward a conclusion: "As birds' wings beat the solid air without which none could fly so words freed by imagination affirm reality by their flight" (150). Some of Williams's most commonly anthologized short poems come from *Spring and All,* which is currently unavailable under separate cover. "The Waste Land" is ubiquitous. Williams was at least partially right to have feared defeat at Eliot's hand. Williams's work did, though, inspire and inform much of the more innovative and experimental poetry of the century, many of the groups and movements with titles that reflect his predilection for the "objective" side of the thing-ness of the image: Louis Zukofsky's and Charles Reznikoff's Objectivism, Charles Olson's Projectivism, Robert Grenier's and Charles Bernstein's L=A=N=G=U=A=G=E poetry, most of the Beat generation, a whole host of Concrete poets, to mention some of the notables. In any case, Williams's "red wheel barrow" poem, number XXII in the book, is both typical and very famous:

> so much depends
> upon
>
> a rcd wheel
> barrow
>
> glazed with rain
> water
>
> beside the white
> chickens (138)

Here is a very good example of a poem that cannot be read through the system of the New Criticism. It seems impervious, almost trivial, from that vantage point. It simply says what it says, a "new object . . . not a mirror up to nature but—." Even to read it in isolation, wrenched from its place in this arrangement, is to miss most of what it has to offer. It is a thing in a field of other things (not just the rest of the twenty-seven poems in the volume but also all the deep, dense, and sometimes wacky prose passages) which, disparate as they might initially seem, interact with one another in quite integral and intimate ways. When Williams later coined the now-famous phrase "no ideas but in things," this is what he had in mind.

❦

THIS PAST WEEKEND MY WIFE AND SON and I took a quick trip to Baltimore, just to get away from our routines here. My sister lives there, so it's a city we know pretty well and there were specific things we wanted to see and do, the usual touristy things, like the magnificent aquarium and the pastoral, now a little disheveled, park-like zoo. Just by happenstance, we found out about the American Visionary Art Museum, the galleries of which are devoted entirely to artists who are self-taught. Since my son is an artist, we decided to visit it. The art there was just disarming, so vivid, playful, somber, charming, funny, dark, strange, almost any kind of effect you can imagine achieved through almost any type or combination of everyday materials you can imagine—painted log animals; yarn cocoons wound around kleptomaniacally acquired objects; small, complex, wooden machines of ducks swimming on the ocean or men galloping on horseback; big sculptures made from mirrors; robots based on circulating fans; painted window screens (a Baltimore invention and tradition)—folk art, rustic art, all made by just ordinary people who had the urge to make something and made it with what was at hand. I'm no expert on art, but, like everyone else, I visit from time to time the kinds of museums designed to house "great" art. I find my experiences there to be both rich and enjoyable, as most people do: not unlike reading a very good book to learn something from it or be edified, educated, even changed by it, as one is by a "knowledgeable" guide. Art of that sort can obviously have a valuable impact on anyone who views it with an attitude of open reception. But it is often more of the commemoration variety. The experience of the American Visionary Art Museum is different. There is no radical distinction, for example, between artist and viewer. My first reaction, in fact, to almost everything I saw was not admiration for a gift and skill beyond mine, but an instinctive desire to try out what the artist was doing with his or her materials, to make a megawood carving of an antlered deer, to paint a rustic scene on a board in the primitive style with bold colors, to take apart a rotating fan, to dab tranquil, idyllic scenes on my window screens. And my second reaction, even to the darker and more depressing pieces or artist biographies, was delight. I don't think there was one person represented who, when she started making her art, would have been able to anticipate, let alone expect, ending up in a gallery. Many of them began making art later in life and most of them were not "discovered" until even later in life or after they died. None of them have made any significant amount of money from their art. Yet all of the work was overwhelmingly laden with vitality, dignity, whimsy, beauty. And I found this to be not only enlivening, even restorative, but inspirational—not in the sense of generating anything like Wordsworth's "thoughts that do lie too deep for tears," which is what "museum-quality" art is capable of and very valuable for, but in building in me an overpowering urge to go off and make something of my own out of the material at hand, which is what Wordsworth does for you when you re-read him not for his great thoughts but for his way of seeing the world and living a life and, perhaps, writing a book of your own, which is what Whitman expressly invites you to do, once you get to the "origin of all poems," that Larissa you can navigate toward by re-reading his work, or that of any other poets you'd like.

Two ❧ The Other Side of Thirty

I N 1971, MY FIRST YEAR OUT OF COLLEGE, I was trying with little success to find some sort of job I might actually be suited for. Generally discouraged, I suppose, about my overall prospects, I took a couple of graduate classes as a part-time student, hoping they might help me figure out a way to bring my interest in poetry into some consonance with my occupational future. One of them was a course on Shakespeare's tragedies. Most of the students were older by some years than my twenty-two. One of them in particular was a man in his late thirties or early forties, hair about shoulder-length, often pulled back in a ponytail, and kind of a belated hippy look in his dress—worn jeans, open shirt. From his demeanor, he seemed like a teacher of some sort, quite well read and confident in his views, unlike me, who had a long record of classroom silence in my academic portfolio, was a bit unsure of myself at the graduate level and, more generally, about "the field" of English studies in the rudimentary and largely wrong-headed ways I was imagining its contours. Early on in our discussions of *King Lear*, already my favorite of Shakespeare's tragedies, this man intoned, with his characteristically baritone air of authority, one which I was both a bit intimidated by and had already concluded was an affectation, this pronouncement: "No one under thirty can *possibly* understand *Lear.*" The thirty-year barrier was, for my generation, a line of demarcation between us and all previous generations, who had been largely dismissed from relevance with the variations of the mantra: "Don't trust anyone over thirty."

I was quite offended by my fellow student's pronouncement, which he explained was based on his belief that certain human experiences available only as one ages—marriage, children, loss, the obvious things we might include under the category of "life"—were necessary in order to fully fathom the decisions that bring Lear to his grief. I thought (but never said): "What difference does it make how old I am? The human condition is the human condition, and I can certainly grasp it in its depths at this age, as I could when I was fifteen or will when I'm eighty-five. Besides, you're obviously over thirty. What do you know? About me, what I've been through already? About anything, really?" Despite my inner protestations, though, that difference between us, and the weight of his imperative, kept nagging at me. In some ways, it ruined *Lear* for me. Every time I've come back to it since, I think of that potential deficiency in my reading—ironically, even now, when I'm twenty or more years older than that man was at the time and certainly carry the necessary baggage he was talking about. His silly statement has stood, stands now, at or near the center of one of the conundrums that interests me as a reader of poetry: "What does biographical age have to do with the process of re-reading?" Only now, I am just as interested in, and troubled by, questions about the age of the poets when they composed the pieces I'm reading as I am by questions about the role of my advancing age as a reader of their works.

That gets me back to Wordsworth, and his beautiful "Ode," in which he says: "The things which I have seen I now can see no more" (331, line 9). I was in my early teens when I first read this poem. I remember how deeply moved I was by what I thought of as the bereft poet's stoic courage in the face of the loss of his creative force. I remember how I pictured him, as a man in his sixties, at least, unsmiling but not severe looking, almost pleasant in his aspect, with a mane of white hair. Maybe there was a picture of that sort in a book I was reading from, though if so it was more likely of Whitman, who was often pictured this way. Maybe I just made that all up based on my impressions of the poem. But that image established itself so firmly in my mind that I have never since been able to read this poem without having it float up first as the author/other with whom I am in conversation as I read. I, on the other hand, thought of myself as what Wordsworth wished he still could be, not just remember being. I don't mean the corny little "Child among his newborn blisses . . . fretted by sallies of his mother's kisses, / with light upon him from his father's eyes!" (332, 85–89), which even then sounded almost laughably naïve to me. It was in section 5 that I located myself, as the one who had come "trailing clouds of glory" (332, 65), only now becoming more and more conscious of the darkening "[s]hades of the prison-house begin[ning] to close" (332, 68). I was, I thought, still "Nature's Priest" with my "vision splendid," though I felt it was being threatened by "the light of common day" (332, 73–77).

I grew up in a small town in a largely rural area. Walk in any direction from my house for a mile, or less, and you'd be in the woods, which is where I went quite often to be alone. There was a specific spot I liked, on a large rock, jutting out into the Lackawanna River. To get to it you had to go down a fairly steep, slippery bank and through some trees whose branches overhung the rock, making it almost invisible from any outside vantage point. While there were no "cataracts blow[ing] their trumpets from the steep" (332, 25) anywhere nearby, the current was swift and the water turbulent enough to inspire my native, romantic sensibilities on a Wordsworthian scale. I'd go off there and sit for what seemed like hours watching the dark water, thinking. I have no recollection about what. But when I read the "Ode," I thought of that spot, of a young Wordsworth having found so many of his own spots over the years, of his going to them to think and then write about "the glory and the dream" (332, 57) as I hoped to be able to do. I felt I still had something like the "visionary gleam" (332, 56) he had lost, that it was, I knew from my end of it, as he did from his end of it, almost by definition perishable and would someday be gone. But not, I thought thankfully, for quite some time, not before I had done what I wanted to do with it, perhaps even using the cautionary aspect of the "Ode" as a way of sustaining it longer, aware as I was, based on my experience and on Wordsworth's, too, of its intrinsically fragile nature, its inevitable tendency to "fade."

As I said, the dynamics of my relationship with Wordsworth, encoded partially in the images inspired by this poem—of him as an elderly man and me as riverside recluse—dominated my reading of the poem for many years, through my graduate work and into my career, unencumbered, largely, by the arsenal of scholarship I was accumulating along the way. It was not until sometime in the mid-1980s that I actually got to teach Wordsworth in a course, through *Lyrical Ballads*, that amazing collection he produced in collaboration with Coleridge. I was preparing for a class focused on "Lines Composed a Few Miles Above Tintern Abbey on Revisiting the Banks of the Wye during a Tour. July 13, 1798," a poem I have always associated closely with the "Ode" in its mood and themes, to the extent that I often misremember from which poems certain loose lines I've memorized actually come. I wanted to talk that day about the profound sense of loss that afflicts Wordsworth, as we know him through this work, about what such a sense of loss might allow us to understand about the Romantic enterprise and about creative endeavors in general, this particular way of conceptualizing them in relation to age, I mean. His is by definition a poem about the aging process and its consequences. It's been five years—"five summers, with the length / Of five long winters!" (301, 1)—since his last visit to this part of the English countryside, and as the poem develops it becomes quite clear that something of magnitude has been lost in the interim, something that can only become fully visible to him by its absence in this re-visit to the same vantage point. This experience is inflected and tinged by recollection: "the picture of the mind" that the current scene "revives," in much the same way evoked in the "Ode" (302, 61).

Present and past become inseparable, establishing a temporal foundation for what, a little later in the poem, will become Wordsworth's broader epistemological assertion of the relationship between sensory perception and imaginative invention: "both what they half create, / And what perceive" (302, 106–7). I wanted to talk about the poet's age and its relation to this change, especially as it impacts the role of his sister, Dorothy, the absent auditor for this poem, a sort of empty space in which we, as readers, can stand to receive and assess whatever wisdom it is that Wordsworth has to offer. Here is Wordsworth, the older brother, standing in this spot he visited five years prior, becoming aware that he has "changed, no doubt, from what I was when first / I came among these hills," (302, 66–67) soliloquizing to his "dearest Friend" in whose voice, her voice, he can "catch / The language of my former heart"; in whom he can for "a little while . . . behold . . . what [he] was once"; his sister, who for him comes immediately to stand for a "Nature" that leads "from joy to joy"; and who, unlike him, is still capable of the "wild ecstacies" that preceded *his* now dominant "sober pleasure" of age (302, 116–39). It is such a gorgeous and expertly crafted poem for deep reflection about the losses associated with maturation, as we stand in the locus of his younger sister, listening.

So I took a look at the dates, just to be sure I'd get the facts right in the process. The poem was composed in 1798, just in time to make it into *Lyri-*

cal Ballads as a sort of concluding capstone. And Wordsworth was born in 1770. So he's twenty-eight here, still comfortably under thirty, the barrier for trustworthiness for my generation. And below my fellow student's cutoff for eligibility to understand *Lear*. Twenty-eight! I was, at the time, almost fifteen years older than that. And because of my mental images of Wordsworth, I still thought I had a way to go before I would be fully afflicted by the "[t]houghts that do often lie too deep for tears" (334, 204) he has to cope with by the time he writes the "Ode." In addition, I discovered that Dorothy, whom I had always imagined as his way-younger kid sister, given the way he positions himself in relation to her, was really only about *a year* younger than he. So I checked again how old he was when he started writing the "Ode." Thirty-two. Old enough now, by my classmate's timeline at least to read *Lear*, but still, so young, younger by years than I was right then. I had along the way, over the years, looked at these dates many times. I "knew" them in a certain way. But they never sank in deep enough to displace my original conception of Wordsworth as the elder statesman of Romanticism, with an emphasis on "elder," this specialist on loss, on finding "[s]trength in what remains behind" (332, 180). From the first time I read Wordsworth, I'd hoped to be like him when I finally got old enough simply to remember, but not to inhabit, my own "clouds of glory." And then I found out I was already way past that point. I was not Lear's peer just yet, but I could certainly sense an imminent threat from that cranky, frantic, ranting shell of a man shambling up over the horizon, urging me to climb in.

Though the key lines in "Tintern Abbey," a little more than halfway through the poem, seem to be the ones that name Nature as the "presence [I have felt] that disturbs me with the joy of elevated thoughts; a sense sublime" (302, 94–95), this is to me much more a poem about, and afflicted by, absences. Wordsworth uses that exact word early in the poem, for example, to characterize the time he has spent between his two journeys to the Wye, and then again at the end of the poem, projecting Dorothy's future time away from the place and its consequences for her. He uses negatives and negations over and over in his figurative constructions—"nots" and "nors" and "no mores" litter the poem, suggesting the "half-extinguished thoughts" that fill him with "a sad perplexity" (302, 58–60). Likewise for the reversals of typical ways for referencing memory: "pleasure" and "acts of kindness and love," for example, are "unremembered" rather than forgotten, and his final plea, twice, to Dorothy is "nor wilt thou then forget" this place, him, their standing together there. Even Dorothy herself is absent to his soliloquy; her primary role is to provide us, as absent overhearers, an empty space to stand in.

This sense of loss, absence, is obviously temperamental for Wordsworth. It creeps in over and over in his work. In his famous sonnet "The World Is Too Much with Us," "we have given our hearts away" and he'd "rather be a Pagan suckled in a creed outworn" (341). In "I Wandered Lonely as a Cloud," the real value of the "ten thousand" daffodils is that they "flash upon that inward eye" "when on my couch I lie / In vacant or in pensive mood" (345). Even in a poem like "The Solitary Reaper," an almost pictorial report of the "solitary Highland Lass," by poem's end he says, "[t]he music in my heart I bore, / Long after it was heard no more" (347).

All of this is made almost inevitable, I think, by the mode of composition he recommends in this famous passage from his preface to *Lyrical Ballads*: "I have said that poetry is the spontaneous overflow of powerful feelings; it takes its origin from emotion recollected in tranquility: the emotion is contemplated till, by a species of re-action, the tranquillity gradually disappears, and an emotion, kindred to that which was before the subject of contemplation, is gradually produced, and does itself actually exist in the mind" (432). When you read this as a poet, you're inevitably thinking: OK, if I want to write a Wordsworth poem, what do I need to do? The Romantic cliché tends to focus on "the spontaneous overflow of powerful feelings" part, a sort of spur-of-the-moment gut-spilling about what you're feeling right here, right now. But that's not Wordsworth's method at all. For him there are multiple displacements away from the original emotion. First, an emotion (previously felt) must be "recollected," and not in its original animated form, but "in tranquility." Then it must be "contemplated," long enough until a *new* "emotion, kindred to that which was before the subject of contemplation, is gradually produced." It is only "in this mood," which is at least two or three removes from the original emotion, that "successful composition generally begins" (432). This, when you try it, turns out to be a pretty good prescription for a poem about loss, including, ultimately, the loss of the ability to write a poem.

Every writer, at one time or another, perhaps, as in my case, at many times, has to deal with one part of the "loss" I always imagined Wordsworth to be afflicted by, the extended "dry spells" during which we are compelled, for whatever reason, to reside, metaphorically, if not actually, "in lonely rooms, and 'mid the din / Of towns and cities" (301, 25–26). It is during these times, quite typically, that I will turn to Wordsworth, and these two poems specifically, to remind myself of both the "remembered" and "unremembered" benefits of my dormant creative enterprise. Several of these fallow phases have been self-induced, and I talk about these in some detail in the final chapter of this book. The one I'm specifically thinking about here occurred in 1971, when "confessionalism"—Robert Lowell, Sylvia Plath, Anne Sexton, John Berryman, W. D. Snodgrass, et al.—was all the rage, with its attendant fascination, even obsession, with suicidal impulses, with the specter of death, or at least the risk of death, and the corresponding valorization of alcohol as a palliative. I was never much of a drinker and got tired of spending time hanging around with writers in bars getting drunk. One night, another aspiring poet at the table said—simply repeating what was in the air at the time, and had been for a number of years—that if you're not risking your life for your art, you're not an artist. I remember thinking how senseless and egocentric that seemed. I had read all the great poems I could get my hands on, thousands and thousands of them extending back over multiple millennia. The poems he and I were making weren't in the same league as these. But even if they were, to pursue a path toward suicidal inebriation for the sake of art seemed simply ludicrous to me. Besides, I at least wanted to *get to* the untrustworthy age of thirty in one piece. I got up and left and never went back to that particular forum. Some months later, as the effects of all this gradually amplified for me in ways I'll describe in chapter four, I stopped writing poetry for what turned out to be several years.

♣

THE ISSUE OF AGE AND WHO GETS to carry its weight most credibly comes up in another way with "The Rime of the Ancient Mariner." The mariner is, presumably, like Coleridge when he wrote the poem, under thirty when he goes through his harrowing ordeal. He is way to the leeward of that when we get to this instantiation of what has been his lifelong compulsion to retell his story "to the man that must hear" it (*Works* 528, 589). Whether this becomes, for a reader, a "tale" that "teach[es]" or is simply ghoulish, sentimental claptrap hinges to a large extent on precisely these matters.

When I read the poem in college, my first classroom experience with it, we had to read a variety of critical responses. One of them in particular (based on comments about the "faults" of the poem that Coleridge himself made in 1830) stuck in my mind because it argued that the poem worked admirably well up until the last six or seven stanzas, which, from this critic's quite dismissive point of view, simply glom onto a pretty good story a dopey moral tag, one unworthy of the poem. The most egregiously offensive lines in that respect were the overtly Christian ones:

> He prayeth well, who loveth well
> Both man and bird and beast.

> He prayeth best, who loveth best,
> All things both great and small;
> For the dear God who loveth us,
> He made and loveth all. (*Works* 529, 612–17)

Seen primarily as a formal element of the poem, this moral is precisely that, a vacuous adage. We've all heard it a million times before, the sum of which has stripped it of any inherent weight. And formally, the lines are too weak to carry the message in the first place, I can see that, as the critic did. But what about the mariner? Doesn't his story invest that tag with legitimacy, significance, as any life story does with whatever adages it purports to embody? That was my question. And like Coleridge's "forethoughtful query" (*Works* 527) it contained the ambition toward my answer.

In the emotional framework of a reading that attributes credence to the mariner in both of his incarnations here—the young man who endures his suffering, the elderly man who reports it—those truisms of Christian ideology seemed to me to be vested with great dignity and authority. The mariner had earned an abiding right to these dicta and filled them with significance, not just by enduring what he had endured (we all have to do that with what comes our way), and not just by learning an important lesson from his experience (most of us do that at least some of the time), but by embodying his truth persistently on behalf of others, especially those, like the wedding guest, who most need and are least likely to appreciate it.

I think by analogy of the phrase "true happiness comes from within," which I heard repeatedly from my mother, among others, while I was growing up. I dismissed it as a bromide. I simply couldn't believe life's true meaning could be reduced to such stock phrases. I thought: when I get to college, I'll read all the philosophy and literature necessary to find out what the real truth about life's happiness is. Such long and deep reading can be very useful, as I hope this book demonstrates. But the process of getting such knowledge from the head into the bones is by no means automatic.

About eighteen years ago, as a result, it turned out (after several years of various misdiagnoses), of a very unlucky alliance between a migraine condition, an inner ear–related balance disorder, and a lot of stress, which produced profound sleep disorders, persistent vertigo, chronic anxiety, and, finally, exhaustion, I had something like what used to be called a "nervous breakdown." The doctors had other names for it, depending on which one I saw and when: depression, anxiety disorder, post-traumatic stress, insomnia, acid reflux, ulcer, or just plain "nothing, it's all in your head." I would have preferred to have had it called by the (now, apparently, unfashionable) term nervous breakdown, even if it wasn't one. At least that is respectably dramatic. In any case, I spent a number of years in a state of inner distress on a scale I was not accustomed to (and I have a pretty good dark streak) and was quite demoralized by. And then many more years recovering slowly, primarily by becoming more knowledgeable about and therefore familiar with the symptoms of my condition, while learning how to change the attitudes and habits that promoted it and aggravated it. It was during this time that I came fully to understand the meaning of the phrase "true happiness comes from within." Because there are times when there is simply no other place it can come from. And when it does come from there, the expression is no longer a cliché. It is filled with moral force.

During that time, I read a variety of poems about loss and recovery that I believed, from my prior experiences with them, would help me to persevere and, perhaps, overcome my inner disorientation. One of them was "The Rime of the Ancient Mariner." I was especially interested in what the wedding guest actually takes away from his encounter with the mariner, whether he was truly changed, rose "a wiser man" on "the morrow morn," as the narrator claims in the poem's final line, or like me was going to need to have the story repeated more than once before it sank in (529, 625). Or, worse, would have to actually endure some great despair in order to get it. I read the whole poem repeatedly, maybe once every six months or so, and it helped me a great deal. That's one point I want to make about some poets—that, in moments of crisis, they can provide, if not guidance, at least some sustenance, primarily by offering the camaraderie of an/other who has endured comparable difficulties with dignity. In this case, the apparent author at hand is the mariner, though one cannot help but feel, in the reading, that he is a sort of mouthpiece for Coleridge, whose life, I suspected long before I knew anything about him, must have been riven at least from time to time by very deep darknesses. The knowledge at stake here has very little to do with the technical aspects of how the poem was made, or even with what it means in a literary sense. It's a deeper and more emotion-laden knowledge about life and how to navigate a proper way through it, a knowledge that derives from an intimate connection between author and reader, art and life. Where could one find a better tale of personal redemption than the ancient mariner's? And how could one imagine the author of the poem, this Coleridge, as someone not intimate himself with at least the fears and afflictions and compulsions, if not the actual physical travails, of his hoary hero?

One of the odd taboos of our culture is the one surrounding mental problems. As unpleasant as it might be, we are at least tolerant of social discourse about all sorts of medical ailments, and we are willing, if not eager, to listen to the descriptions of symptoms and procedures, no matter how gory or invasive the details. But psychological problems are not among those ailments. There's an old Arlo Guthrie song called "Alice's Restaurant," sort of an anthem of the sixties. At one point in the (very long) song, Guthrie says in quite a funny way, describing the scene of his draft physical: "And they all moved away from me on the bench." That's kind of what it feels like when you are having psychological problems. The opening stanzas of the "Rime" remind me a little of "Alice's Restaurant" in this respect:

> It is an ancient Mariner,
> And he stoppeth one of three.
> "By thy long grey beard and glittering eye,
> Now wherefore stopp'st thou me?
>
> The Bridegroom's doors are opened wide,
> And I am next of kin;
> The guests are met, the feast is set:
> May'st hear the merry din."
>
> He holds him with his skinny hand,
> "There was a ship," quoth he.
> "Hold off! unhand me, grey-beard loon!'
> Eftsoons his hand dropt he.
>
> He holds him with his glittering eye—
> The Wedding-Guest stood still,
> And listens like a three years' child:
> The Mariner hath his will. (520–21, 1–16)

Right off the bat, the mariner is constructed as a weird and unwelcome oddball. The wedding guest is on his actual way to the actual ceremony and is not in the least inclined to brook any interruption, let alone one from this "graybeard loon." The mariner does nothing to ameliorate this perception. He "holds him with his skinny hand" and then, when he's told to let go, which he does "eftsoons" (what a great word), he holds him instead "with his glittering eye," transfixing the wedding guest, who, against his will, must listen "like a three years' child." So the story opens with a double dose of strangeness and estrangement, and as readers we are not just invited but almost compelled to share the infantilized wedding guest's irritation and frustration for having been waylaid by such a creepy crackpot.

What follows is the mariner's gripping tale of adventure and misadventure, guilt and expiation on an almost unimaginable scale. As the trip to the Southern ocean opens, the mariner is, apparently, young and ordinary, just another hand on deck. They are "chased . . . south" by storms and get caught up in mist and snow, and finally ice (521, 44). An albatross arrives, seeming to bring with it a "good south wind" that helps get them out of their predicament (521, 71). Then, for no apparent reason, the mariner shoots the bird—cast here as a "Christian soul" that the crew had hailed "in God's name"—with his crossbow (521, 65–66). That we are offered no motive whatsoever for this act, leaving it entirely dark in the narrative, is, to me, key to making this poem work in the ways it works for me. We all act similarly capriciously from time to time. We have an unaccountable urge to do something, and we do it, right then, without bothering at the moment to take full account, sometimes *any* account, of the potential consequences. One just does things. And there are consequences. That is part of the horror and glory of life.

The crew first reacts negatively to the mariner's killing the bird, then positively, their judgments following fickly the changes of weather. The social component of the mariner's penalty is important here, as an element of the more private and personal moral component: He "had done a hellish thing, / And it would work 'em woe" (522, 91–92). As it certainly does. Big time. There is a kind of over-the-top quality to the whole operation that really appealed to me as a teenager, and appeals to me still, this all-or-nothing moral landscape. Most people probably perceive me a fairly steady, low-key kind of person, not prone to overreaction or dramatics. And, on the outside, I suppose I am all that, quite genuinely, a public persona built up over the long haul by a series of choices and imperatives. But inside is a different story. There, it's an ongoing battle, epic in scale, lots of black and white, victories and defeats, and inordinately out of proportion moral forces grinding the gears forward. Part of this for me is due to my 1950s-vintage Catholic upbringing—that lovely mix of funny lines and petrifying fear. I think of Garrison Keillor's joking name for the local Catholic church in Lake Wobegon: Our Lady of Perpetual Responsibility. Part of it is probably due to my family's Slovenian/Irish heritage (both cultures combine moral gravity and humor in interesting ways) and to the place where I grew up, an anthracite-mining town after the coal had run out. In any case, I was well positioned by cultural forces to get the mariner's message right from the outset. He did something stupid, quite witlessly, and he had to pay the price. The price detailed in the poem is pretty steep—the subsequent death of all his deckhands, the horror of the dice-throw that LIFE-IN-DEATH wins to get to torture him further on his journey "home," the eerie final stages of the trip with his mates, enspirited, steering the ship in silence, their accusing eyes riveted on him, the catastrophic collapse in the harbor, the rickety ship being sucked into a maelstrom. But really, to me, it was just like everyday life. One's soul is at stake, a mistake is made, there are consequences.

How does the mariner recover from his mistake? Well, he starts, spiritually, mid-poem, when "A spring of love" gushes from his heart and he "blesse[s] . . . unaware" the water snakes that "coiled and swam" around the ship. Then he "could pray," and the albatross "fell off" his neck, where the other mariners hung it, originally, to mark his sin (524, 280–91). Finally, he sleeps and drinks:

> Oh sleep! it is a gentle thing,
> Beloved from pole to pole!
> To Mary Queen the praise be given!
> She sent the gentle sleep from Heaven,
> That slid into my soul.
>
> The silly buckets on the deck,
> That had so long remained,
> I dreamt that they were filled with dew;
> And when I awoke, it rained. (524–25, 292–300)

I used to read these lines sometimes when I couldn't sleep for days on end. This whole section of Coleridge's poem, the end of part IV and beginning of part V, is beyond compare, I think, for catharsis, an overwhelming sense of deep relief. It is why I read the poem when I need to. If the mariner can come back from his nightmare, so, I believe, can I. That mine, like his, will remain in some respects as a sort of chronic affliction, arising "at an uncertain hour" as a story that needs to be told, if only to myself, well, that makes it all the better (528, 582).

The combination of fear and distrust that is often inspired by obvious symptoms of mental imbalance is captured beautifully at the end of the poem as the mariner is drawn out of the whirling drink into the pilot's boat. He, along with his son and the "Hermit good" come to the mariner's rescue, much to their immediate chagrin:

> I moved my lips—the Pilot shrieked
> And fell down in a fit;
> The holy Hermit raised his eyes,
> And prayed where he did sit.

> I took the oars: the Pilot's boy,
> Who now doth crazy go,
> Laughed loud and long, and all the while
> His eyes went to and fro.
> "Ha! ha!" quoth he, "full plain I see,
> The Devil knows how to row." (528, 560–9)

Insanity here is a kind of contagion. Maybe that's what so discomfiting about being around it, the underlying fear we share with the Pilot's boy that we might be insanely "spun round and round," drawn with the mariner's ship "down like lead," never to resurface (528, 549, 557).

This gets us back to the contested closing moral tags of the poem. Clichés these are, of course, but indexed to the poem itself, the world it builds, they do, for me at least, come freighted with legitimate weight. It is the mariner's arbitrary act of violence that initiates his ordeal, the sort of thing a brash, young man might do without a moment's thought. And then he finds himself at the depth of his misery,

> Alone, alone, all, all alone,
> Alone on a wide wide sea!
> And never a saint took pity on
> My soul in agony.

> The many men, so beautiful!
> And they all dead did lie:
> And a thousand thousand slimy things
> Lived on; and so did I. (524, 232–39)

It is here that his attention is riveted by those "water snakes" (524, 273):

> They moved in tracks of shining white,
> And when they reared, the elfish light
> Fell off in hoary flakes.
>
> Within the shadow of the ship
> I watched their rich attire:
> Blue, glossy green, and velvet black,
> They coiled and swam; and every track
> Was a flash of golden fire.
>
> O happy living things! no tongue
> Their beauty might declare:
> A spring of love gushed from my heart,
> And I blessed them unaware:
> Sure my kind saint took pity on me,
> And I blessed them unaware. (524, 274–87)

This final six-line stanza, one of only a few in the poem, and right in its middle, so poignant and moving, is enough in its own right (though the poem offers more) to invest the closing with significance: the evidence, in effect, that supports the conclusion. Suffice it to say, that if we have indeed allowed ourselves to stand in the wedding guest's place—to experience his initial bristling irritation at having been waylaid from such an important occasion; to experience the frustration of being so hypnotized by the mariner's captivating powers of speech; to experience the deep fear and grief as well as the ultimate release from the grip of death itself that the ghastly tale embodies; to experience all of these wild, over the top, gloomy and glamorous, and almost (but not quite) frightfully comic ramblings—then we will know exactly what the mariner means by his impassioned injunction to pray and love, and it will make a difference in how we go through the day, and the next, as it did for the wedding guest:

> He went like one that hath been stunned,
> And is of sense forlorn:
> A sadder and a wiser man,
> He rose the morrow morn. (529, 622–25)

♣

BETWEEN 1853 AND 1855 SOMETHING, or some things, happened to transform Walter Whitman, middling journalist and occasional dandy, into "Walt Whitman, an American, one of the roughs, a kosmos" (54, 498). Transformations of this sort can never, from an external point of view, most especially at such a historical remove (despite, I would argue, the most aggressive and diligent pursuits of critics and historians), be fully explained or accounted for. Even if Whitman had told us, which he didn't, we would be hard pressed to balance the accounts, one side of the divide to the other, the transformation seems so incommensurably complete.

With Whitman, the gap between what we know about him and what he did is especially large. But it is a fact that Whitman was in his mid-thirties, a bit to the topside of the *Lear*-reading eligibility line, when, by writing his first book, under a title that (in an uncharacteristic, and final, act of verbal economy) would suffice him for the rest of his life: *Leaves of Grass*, he provided a heroic model for the male mid-life crisis (should I buy a Harley or write the best poem of the century? Hmmm . . .) and, in the process, re-made himself. One way of reading the poem is as a map of this crisis: identity problems, megalomania, paroxysms of sex, some Eastern philosophy, a preoccupation with death, the whole nine yards. Coming better to understand his inner dynamics required my getting closer to that stage myself, not quite past thirty, the line of demarcation announced by my fellow student in the Shakespeare class, but at least into my adulthood. And I feel as if I understand him better and better as I get older, most especially so in the process of having to traverse, as all of us who last long enough must, the travails of middle age.

Identity-formation (or -transformation) is, almost by definition, one of the things that eludes explanation and, often, even comprehension. All of us change consequentially, even dramatically, over time. Sometimes, that time can be quite compact—a day, a week, a year. We go in as one person and come out as another. The last half century or so has been preoccupied with identity-related matters to an extreme, from the the tendencies of the 1960s, encoded in terms like "expressivism" and "authenticity," to the rise in the 1980s and '90s, of poststructuralist and social constructionist critiques of the essentialist self. One time frame that I think can compare with ours in that regard is Whitman's, most especially the period prior to the Civil War: the epic expansion of the country westward, the turmoil surrounding slavery, the ambient influence of Transcendentalism. In the midst of this stew, Whitman remade himself into a poet, an epic poet, an American poet, *the* American poet, a seer, and, yes, a character, in all of the better or worse implications of that term. How do we know this? He wrote *Leaves of Grass*, most especially the "leaf" that he later called "Song of Myself," as an artifactual re-presentation not so much, perhaps, of the process of his remaking, though we can see sketchy outlines of it, as of its effects. In it, he declares:

> Clear and sweet is my soul . . . . and clear and sweet is all that is
>   not my soul.
> Lack one lacks both . . . . and the unseen is proved by the seen,
> Till that becomes unseen and receives proof in its turn. (30, 44–6)

"Soul" is a term we use relatively commonly in everyday discourse, but almost always in the most vacuous ways: "heart and soul," "soul mates," "soul" music; even in religious discourse, the term tends to be stripped of any particular spiritual urgency, let alone any immediate application to everyday life. The mode of Catholicism in which I was raised was, as I've said, a wry combination of, on the one hand, scaring the crap out of you with an overwhelming sense of potential evil, and one's inclination to sin, and one's responsibility in the face of such a dynamic; and then, on the other, coming up with a joke about it all to make you laugh and forget about it, in large part because the premise of the scary part is just untenable at the level of human enterprise over the long haul. I was temperamentally pretty intense by nature, so this dark and funny spirituality found some fertile ground there. I ended up spending a lot of time as a child and adolescent thinking about my soul, what it was, what I needed to be doing with and for it, etc. Part of the appeal of poetry, as I've suggested, was my sense that it impacted my actual soul, educated me, in the sense of enlightening me to what my capacities might be if I were to inhabit my soul in a more deeply or fully human way.

When I first read Whitman, I had not yet read any Plato. But I had a very strong sense that the literature I was reading went directly to my core—in exactly the way that Socrates describes to Hippocrates in *Protagoras*, when warning him about the sort of ultimate risks inherent in choosing a mentor:

> But what is it that nourishes a soul?
>   What it learns, presumably, I said. . . . But knowledge cannot be
> taken away in a parcel. When you have paid for it you must receive

it straight into the soul. You go away having learned it and are benefited or harmed accordingly. So I suggest we give this matter some thought, not only by ourselves, but also with those who are older than we . . . (313–14, 313c–14b)

I believed that the literature I read had a permanent effect on who "I" was, one from which I could not recover simply through willed forgetfulness, though my "I" back then would have had no quotation marks around it. I was a through-and-through essentialist (as to some extent, despite my best efforts and the best efforts of two generations of critical theory, in which I have been imbued, I'm sure I still am), deeply vested in a sense of the uniqueness, integrity, and inwardly-centeredness of a "self" that was incontrovertibly mine, and a fully committed adherent to what M. H. Abrams called the "lamp" metaphor for human perception and invention—the light of the soul spilling out to illuminate the world—though I hadn't yet read Abrams, either. I had, though, spent enough time with two of his primary examples—Wordsworth and Coleridge—to have absorbed the most commonplace version of their epistemic systems. Identity was endowed, fixed and durable. I liked mine and I liked it the way it was. I didn't like Whitman's and I didn't like his approach to me: all that swagger and braggadocio threatening to impinge on my inner life. I had no problem with doing the tasks I was asked perform at school, at home, at work. But I hated any effort to assert even a modest measure of control over my private world of thoughts, emotions, ideas. Such moves, I believed, infringed at the level of self and soul, and from that I protected myself—and my soul.

I read Walt Whitman's "Song of Myself" for the first time in my sophomore year in high school, in the midst of a unit on American literature in my English class. I had already been immersed in more traditional modes of poetry: Poe first of all, whose work I had spent my nights memorizing; Coleridge, likewise; Wordsworth; Keats; an assortment of like-minded others. I had developed on the basis of that reading a very clear idea of what a poem was, what it was fit for, and what it could be designed to do. Our teacher, Mrs. Dunleavy, so plain-seeming and conservative in every visible respect, as unlikely a Whitmanian as one could imagine, read the first three lines of "Song of Myself" aloud in class. The impact was so intense I can actually remember where I was sitting in the room, what the book looked like in front of me, the sound of the teacher's lilting voice intoning:

I celebrate myself,
And what I assume you shall assume,
For every atom belonging to me as good belongs to you. (28, 1–3)

I was immediately overwhelmed with aggravation, almost revulsion. "This is not a poem," I thought. It didn't scan, it didn't rhyme. I had studied these things on my own in hopes of being able to write poems myself, and (I thought) I knew what a poem was supposed to sound like. So *how* Whitman was saying what he had to say bothered me quite a lot. Those opening lines sounded to me like straight prose. Beyond that, and more importantly in relation to my reaction, was *what* he was saying. This "I" who was celebrating himself: What for? And what about? Who cares about his self-celebrations anyway? And why should I even consider allowing what *he* assumed to become what I assumed? This was the most unmitigated gall, as I saw it, and not to be tolerated from a poet. Endorsing the express project of the third line—this interchange of atoms—was simply out of the question for me. You and I, Walt, becoming one at the atomic level? Not bloody likely. In short, I concluded very quickly that Whitman was not someone I wanted to be spending much time with, let alone lending my soul to. So I entered into my "school" reading mode, whereby the material at hand went into a very safe repository for storage and retrieval purposes only. I could hold it there long enough to take tests and answer questions. Then, when the assessment was done, I could dump it. I had set up such a holding pen almost instinctively over the years, as a way of preventing the deleterious effects about which Plato warns us. I still have it and use it all the time for things I don't want to allow to become durably a part of "me." I started reading "Song of Myself" in that mode immediately after those first three lines. The efficacy of my method is evidenced by the difference in impact I can recall between the first three lines, which are burned into my memory, and the remainder of the poem, from the reading of which, on that occasion at least, I cannot recall one detail.

I read "Song of Myself" for the second time in college, in an American lit course, with somewhat better results. This time, I actually learned a lot about Whitman, about his technique and his process, and was able to make good use of that information in understanding his contemporary successors, like Allen Ginsberg, who wrote with a deep debt to Whitman. But despite that seemingly provident convergence between his literary heirs, whom I understood quite well, and their primary source, I still didn't get what

Whitman was about. Not at least in the way I had been so easily able to do with Coleridge. There is, I believe, no way to really receive what Whitman proffers without being willing to stand fully in the set of shoes that he leaves behind for us as he ambles through the poem—not his shoes, precisely, because that would be counter to his project in the poem—just shoes that don't quite fit right until you walk in them for a while. I was simply not yet able to do this for and with Whitman. Relationships with poets are, as I said, much like our other social relationships. In some, we hit it off right from the start. Others take time. In the case of Whitman, for me, it just took a lot of time. This sort of persistence can pay off quite handsomely for any reader of poets, and I highly recommend it. The further afield a poet at first seems, the harder you must work to traverse the distances between. You don't necessary learn *more* than you would from an immediately companionable spirit, but you do tend to learn some things you are less inclined to find out on your own.

One of the things I noticed and approved of during this contact with Whitman was how much difficulty we had in talking about his poems through the lens of the New Criticism, which I was coming to both understand and abhor—self-consciously rather than tacitly—as a historically produced critical system. That the essence of Whitman's enterprise eluded this critical system almost entirely enhanced his appeal for me. Still, my rapprochement with Whitman was more like Pound's pretty lame "Pact" than a real conversion:

> I make a pact with you, Walt Whitman—
> I have detested you long enough.
> I come to you as a grown child
> Who has had a pig-headed father;
> I am old enough now to make friends.
> It was you that broke the new wood,
> Now is a time for carving.
> We have one sap and one root—
> Let there be commerce between us. (*Lustra* 21)

Like Pound, I understood that there was at least the possibility for some "commerce between us," but unlike Pound, who saw himself as the carver, the real artificer for the new wood laid out by his "pig-headed father" (ah! the tact and grace of Pound!), I really *did* want to think about the "soul" part of "Song of Myself" and how it might apply to me. I just couldn't see right then how to do it.

I was in the right place, though, a small Jesuit college that was a hotbed of political activism, at about the right time, the late 1960s, to pursue such an inquiry. The moral theory I was exploring in my philosophy and theology classrooms (much of it, in the latter case, via the deeply authoritarian traditions of the Catholic Church) provided a pretty stiff spine for the much more amorphous anti-establishment tendencies of the loosely affiliated political action movements (civil rights, anti-war, draft resistance, feminist) emerging around me and in which I began to participate outside of the classroom. I thought I had found in Whitman a companionable sponsor for my evolving thinking about matters of the soul, one who would provide a space both for my deep sense of reverence for things spiritual, my Strelnikov-like stringency on matters of political principle, and my lapsed, but still ticking, Catholic ideology. I can now see just how much I had in common with Pound, when he "found" *his* Whitman. Much of it is not very appealing from this distant vantage point. Perhaps that was the case for Pound as he waited—more like a pig-headed child than the father of Modernist poetics—locked up in an American military detention center near Pisa, Italy, because of his pro-Fascist broadcasts on Radio Rome during World War II, watching ants and struggling with "vanity" as he wrote the poignant and haunting *Pisan Cantos.*

Around this time I was also reading a lot of Yeats, who approaches soul-related matters persistently and directly throughout his career. They are built into his system, both the hard-core Catholicism that was part of his cultural baggage and the more esoteric and arcane system for exploring the cycles of the human soul that he published under the title *A Vision,* the content of which apparently derived from a series of automatic writing episodes during which his wife, George, was possessed by a spiritual force, giving it voice through her hand. I did read *A Vision* back then, but mostly with dazed puzzlement. It was the poems that gripped me most firmly, as they still do. Take for one obvious example (though you could close your eyes and randomly pick a poem from his later works, especially, and come up with one that had at least some connection to this issue) a poem like "A Dialogue of Self and Soul." Yeats is in his mid-sixties as he writes "A Dialogue," struggling still with mortality-related problems that had afflicted him in one guise or another almost from the outset. He's not only eligible to read Lear, he could *be* Lear. He's got the years under his belt, but also the temperament for it, stubborn and contentious. Part of his ongoing struggle, it seems to me, has been that his "self" and his "soul," large and rich as each was, never got along too well with one another, and he was quite conscious of, and honest about, their differences. In the heat of their battles, poem after poem got forged. "A Dialogue" appears in his 1933 collection *The Winding Stair and Other Poems*. Of the poems in this collection the most famous is "Byzantium," which ends with my favorite Yeats image: "That dolphin-torn, that gong-tormented sea" (*SP* 140). That poem's second stanza includes the chilling "Shade more than man, more image than a shade" that he calls "death-in-life and life-in-death" (139), which brings to mind (mine at least) the scene in Coleridge's "Rime" where the spirits throw dice to see who gets to do what to whom. The difference between Yeats and the mariner is that Yeats intends to have a say in the outcome, and he believes he can. So there's an austerity and severity to the presentation that is not typical of, or pertinent for, the "Rime." But Yeats's argument in "A Dialogue" is, in the end, irresolute and inconclusive, riven through by the stark, already familiar-to-me binaries that attracted me to him in the first place, the very ones from which I was seeking to escape. I wanted to have a sense of the human value of my soul, but not if its primary ambition was to deliver me from "the crime of death and birth" (131) and from the spiritual value of my "self." But there is really no way to think oneself out of this conundrum through the Irish-Catholic inflected discourse that Yeats and I happened to share.

JAMES WRIGHT, TALKING ABOUT HIGH SCHOOLERS playing football, writes:

> Their sons grow suicidally beautiful
> At the beginning of October,
> And gallop terribly against each other's bodies. (113)

The "beautiful" side of suicide was in the air in the late 1960s, and the same kind of terrible gallop was going on among poets. Three new-to-me poets I encountered around that time provided me some indirect guidance about the inside-out or outside-in conundrum I had already been thinking about through the methodological argument between William Carlos Williams with T. S. Eliot that I describe in chapter 1, as well as a less moralistic framework for thinking about matters of self and soul. The specific books I was reading were Sylvia Plath's *Ariel* (1965), James Wright's *The Branch Will*

Not Break (1963), and Gary Snyder's *Riprap* (1959). All of these poets were right around the age of thirty when they were working on these poems. But their methods, and their fates, were quite different: Sylvia Plath, writing in a mode that the critic M. L. Rosenthal had just tagged "confessional," was the consummate inside-out poet; James Wright, writing in a mode that the poet Robert Bly later called "leaping poetry," was designing a mode of outside-in poetry, based on his readings of European and Latin American surrealists; Gary Snyder, emerging from his early affiliation with the Beat poets, was investing an offshoot of projectivism with his deep immersion in Zen Buddhism.

Ariel contains some astonishing and deservedly now-canonized poems, which accomplish things I had never quite seen before: the austere, eerily quiet, almost lifelessly beautiful "Morning Song," its images like the "hammered gold" in Yeats's poem "Sailing to Byzantium," but so jarringly out-of-place in a poem about a mother and her child in the hospital just after birth (1); or the tight, violent, Holocaust-emblazoned "Lady Lazarus," blurring cultural, family, and personal destinies in its "Dying / is an art" tableau (7). But the poem that most amazed me back then was the more conventional-looking (longer lines, regular stanzas) "Tulips." Look at some of these images from a poem that is saturated with them:

> I am nobody; I have nothing to do with explosions.
> . . . .
> The nurses pass and pass, they are no trouble,
> They pass the way gulls pass inland in their white caps . . .
>
> . . . .
> My body is a pebble to them, they tend it as water
> Tends to pebbles it must run over, smoothing them gently.
>
> . . . .
> I have let things slip, a thirty-year-old cargo boat
> Stubbornly hanging on to my name and address
>
> . . . .
> The tulips are too red in the first place, they hurt me.
> Even through the gift paper I could hear them breathe
> Lightly, through their white swaddlings, like an awful baby.
> Their redness talks to my wounds, it corresponds.
>
> . . . .

> The vivid tulips eat my oxygen.
>
> . . . .
>
> The tulips should be behind bars like dangerous animals;
> They are opening like the mouth of some great African cat. (10–12)

Evident here is an extreme mode of the inside-out approach. Plath, lying in the hospital bed, reduces herself repeatedly to in-animation, like the pebble or the cargo boat. The tulips, on the other hand, take on a garish, scary animation that has no connection with their status as flowers. At one point they even become "an awful baby." Eliot's lilacs seem tame and consoling by comparison. This inversion of our most commonplace distinctions between subjective "things" and objective "things" recurs repeatedly in *Ariel*. In "Morning Song," for example, Plath's own newborn child is "like a fat gold watch," a "new statue." And Plath is:

> . . . no more your mother
> Than the cloud that distils a mirror to reflect its own slow
> Effacement at the wind's hand. (1)

It is hard to imagine a more lifeless and disembodied pair. In other poems, inanimate things become full of life: the "Frost on a leaf . . . talking and cackling" (2); "The train" that "leaves a line of breath" (3); the "late mouths" of the poppies that "cry open" (19). Page after page the world is turned inside-out in the most gripping, disturbing, unnerving, even frightening ways. That inversion is not the only source of power in Plath's method, but it's a significant one. And when we enter her realm, we have an experience of the turmoil and torment she endured there.

Plath is the first female poet I've talked about in any detail so far, which says a lot about how male-dominated the genre was up until this time. Over the next generation, the balance of power in this regard shifted dramatically. By the early 1970s books by women poets were entering the review stream quite routinely. I remember, for example, reviewing Plath's austere and haunting *Winter Trees* in tandem with Anne Sexton's lovely-scary, fairy-tale based *Transformations* in 1972. And that was just the beginning. By the 1990s, many, maybe most, of the poets of historical consequence, both in terms of quality and public recognition, were women. How did this happen? Certainly, part of it was cultural, driven by the gender-equalizing engine of feminism and the women's rights movement. Another part of it was the shift in critical ideologies that occurred in the 1970s. Modernism and the New Criticism, when viewed in retrospect, seem precisely designed to function as patriarchal systems. Both the concept of the "universal" reader or the "impersonal" author can be exposed very quickly as veiled male-gendered modes of authorization. One of the obvious consequences of this was the diminution of female poets. Hilda Doolittle—whom Pound re-named H. D., speaking of male modes of authorization—for example, ended up being pigeon-holed as a skilled but minor imagist. She was not even *included* in the *Norton Anthology* I used in my first college English class. When I finally started to read her work, I was stunned. How could a poet of this magnitude be shunted off on a side rail? Were she writing in our time instead of hers, I think she'd be, if not at the top of the scale, certainly among the highest luminaries; her talent and output are of that level of consequence. The final part of this tectonic shift was made possible by great female poets who emerged to prominence almost in unison during the 1960s, including Plath's flamboyant confessional colleague Anne Sexton, who brought the female body into her poetry in such depth and detail that her work inspired passionate critiques about her subject matter—menstruation and abortion, for example—or her overall tenor. The life and death stakes of the confessional enterprise certainly added a strong spiritual element—at least on my side of the relationships—to their work. But "soul" was not a term that they turned to with any regularity to think through these problems. Especially for the women, this was a poetic of the body, the embodied or disembodied self, in a much more private, psychological sense than Whitman's. And their work, along with that of the other women coming to prominence in this era—Adrienne Rich and Denise Levertov come immediately to mind—was crucial in opening up this new "body" of work for the flood of subsequent writers who have flourished in their wake.

One of the vehicles for the evolution to a more gender-balanced marketplace in American poetry was the "deep image," a term Jerome Rothenberg and Robert Kelly coined in the 1960s to describe the poetry of Diane Wakoski, among others. The most prominent guru of this movement was Robert Bly (who, ironically, became even more notorious for his male-celebrating *Iron John*, published in 1990). One of the most famous practitioners of this method was James Wright, though I had no historical sense of any of this when I first read him. *The Branch Will Not Break* was his transitional book from the more traditional, Frostian verse he had been writing in the 1950s to a much freer, more experimental style. Look at these images from a couple of poems in that book:

> The moon drops one or two feathers into the field.
> The dark wheat listens.
>
> . . . .
>
> There they are, the moon's young, trying
> Their wings.
>
> . . . .
>
> Cribs loaded with roughage huddle together
> Before the north clouds.
> The wind tiptoes between poplars.
> The silver maple leaves squint
> Toward the ground. (127)

On the face of it, Wright seems to be enlivening the inanimate much as Plath does. But even the most casual reading will sense a profound difference in method here. These are images that work from the outside in, from perception to the dreamlike states they inspire. Just around this time, Wright was translating poems from a variety of European, mostly Spanish, and Latin American poets and evolved from that basis a hybrid of surrealism, one that makes its initial contact in the natural world, which provokes a turn inward toward the deep image. Robert Bly identifies the key to this method as being attuned to "the inner life of objects" (4), which promotes "a long floating leap": "That leap can be described as a leap from the conscious to the unconscious and back again, a leap from the known part of the mind to the unknown part and back to the known" (1). In other words, in this sort of dream-poem, the integrity of the objects that initiate the leap is ultimately maintained, which is not at all what happens in Plath's poems. Here are some good examples of this type of imagery in Wright's famous poem, "The Blessing:"

> Just off the highway to Rochester, Minnesota,
> Twilight bounds softly forth on the grass.
> And the eyes of those two Indian ponies
> Darken with kindness.
>
> . . . .
>
> I would like to hold the slenderer one in my arms,
>
> . . . .
>
> She is black and white,
> Her mane falls wild on her forehead,
> And the light breeze moves me to caress her long ear

That is delicate as the skin over a girl's wrist.
Suddenly I realize
That if I stepped out of my body I would break
Into blossom. (135)

There are leaps in and back out again throughout this poem, mostly gentle ones. But there's a lot of hard darkness in Wright's work, too, in keeping with the times. Again, soul was not a concept these poets relied on very often, but there was a death-presence intrinsic to the method, quite unlike the one that afflicted the confessionals. *Duende*, a hard-to-translate-to-English term that Bly borrows from the Spanish poet Federico Garcia Lorca, is one of its conceptual loci. As Bly explains: "Duende involves a kind of elation when death is present in the room, it is associated with 'dark' sounds, and when a poet has duende inside him, he brushes past death with each step, and in that presence associates fast" (29). Such dark sounds echo throughout Wright's work. For example, a long, descriptive poem about the placid scene around him as he is "Lying in a Hammock at William Duffy's Farm in Pine Island, Minnesota"—with a "bronze butterfly," cowbells, a chicken hawk "looking for home"—concludes with this jarring leap: "I have wasted my life" (114). The poem from which the book's title is drawn, where "a brilliant blue jay is springing up and down, up and down / on a branch," letting the poet know "That the branch will not break" (125), is the second of a duo of poems called "Two Hangovers," the first of which is much bleaker and more disconsolate, full of images like these:

Locusts and poplars change to unmarried women
Sorting slate from anthracite
Between railroad ties:
The yellow-bearded winter of the depression
Is still alive somewhere, an old man
Counting his collection of bottle caps
In a tarpaper shack under the cold trees
Of my grave. (124)

But Wright's outside-in method must have shed just enough light for him to hold off the moment's death threats, the ones to which Plath ultimately accedes, in body, at least, if not soul.

It is hard to talk about Gary Snyder's work now without getting caught up in all the baggage of his personal journey: His early encounters with

Zen Buddhism that led to extended and earnest study at Buddhist temples in Japan; his translations from the Chinese; his extensive travels through the South Pacific and Middle East, living now and then in remote places with exotic people; his relationship with Jack Kerouac that made him the basis for the main character in *The Dharma Bums*; his relationship with Allen Ginsberg that led to his participation in the legendary Six Gallery reading in San Francisco in 1955; his environmentalism; and on and on. Much of this baggage had already been accrued by the time he published *Riprap* at the age of twenty-nine. Fortunately, I wasn't aware of it when I first ran across the book. In some ways, I wish I hadn't come to know all of this in the meantime. The simple, elegant beauty of the poems seemed to recede further and further from the center of attention—though Snyder kept writing them—as the myth evolved. Here are some lines from the title poem of *Riprap*. Try to imagine reading it, along with the rest of the simple, luminescent others in the book, cold, without any knowledge of the stuff I just mentioned, as a very young man, at a moment of cultural crisis, near collapse, on a scale I've not seen since in my lifetime, in the midst of a poetic ambience that seemed so often to favor death over life, when you're looking for some clarity about the way words might at least explore, even promote, body-soul relationships and not expecting to find it, not at least in a little book you just picked up for reasons you can't even now remember:

> Lay down these words
> Before your mind like rocks.
>   placed solid, by hands
> In choice of place, set
> Before the body of the mind
>   in space and time:
> Solidity of bark, leaf, or wall
>   riprap of things:
> ·
> . . . each rock a word
>   a creek-washed stone
> Granite: ingrained
>   with torment of fire and weight
> Crystal and sediment linked hot
>   all change, in thoughts,
> As well as things. (404)

When Pound first started messing around with his concept of the image, he was, like Snyder, translating some poems from the Chinese, which ended up in a volume called *Cathay*, published in 1915. He was guided in this work by the insights of an American professor working in Japan, Ernest Fenollosa. Fenollosa believed that the Chinese ideogram was a unique kind of linguistic symbol because it had a pictographic component to it, thereby embodying the object to which it pointed in its graphic structure. For Pound, this became the perfect emblem for his concept of the image: a fusion of word with thing. Fenollosa's work was soon discredited, and Snyder, in a 1992 interview with the *Paris Review,* takes pains to distance himself from Pound's conception of the ideogram. You can see notable differences along those lines when you compare Snyder's images with Pound's "In a Station of the Metro" (which appeared first in *Poetry*, April 1913, and became as iconic in Modernist lore as Eliot's "patient etherized upon a table" from "Prufrock" or Williams's "red wheel barrow"):

> The apparition of these faces in the crowd:
> Petals on a wet, black bough. (1)

Pound's image, for example, has an almost clumsy Western duality to it: The faces, the petals. And the faces themselves, at the core of the image, are not vivid but apparitional. In Snyder's poem, there is more of a fusion, not by means of something like Wright's leap between (outer) thing and (inner) dream, but at the level of words laid down "Before your mind like rocks. . . . Before the body of the mind / in space and time." The image has come full circle here, back to its Eastern roots, but informed now by full immersion and sustained practice, not just by Snyder, but by the intervening generations of poets influenced by Pound's simple idea.

Sometimes you find what you want in a place you never meant to look, as was the case with me and Gary Snyder; sometimes you miss what you need when it's right in front of you. Oddly enough, for example, Whitman, whom I was reading for my course, unlike many of the contemporary poets I was connecting with, provided a powerful way of thinking about body and soul as intimately intertwined with one another, almost interchangeable. I just couldn't fully grasp it at the time. As in these lines:

> I am the poet of the body,
> And I am the poet of the soul.

The pleasures of heaven are with me, and the pains of hell are with
me,
The first I graft and increase upon myself . . . . the latter I translate
into a new tongue. (50, 422–25)

Or these:

I have said that the soul is not more than the body,
And I have said that the body is not more than the soul,
And nothing, not God, is greater to one than one's-self is . . .
(93, 1261–63)

Or these:

A gigantic beauty of a stallion, fresh and responsive to my caresses,
Head high in the forehead and wide between the ears,
Limbs glossy and supple, tail dusting the ground,
Eyes well apart and full of sparkling wickedness . . . . ears finely cut
and flexibly moving.

His nostrils dilate . . . . my heels embrace him . . . . his well built
limbs tremble with pleasure . . . . we speed around and return.

I but use you a moment and then I resign you stallion . . . . and do
not need your paces, and outgallop them,
And myself as I stand or sit pass faster than you.

Swift wind! Space! My Soul! Now I know it is true what I guessed at;
What I guessed when I loafed on the grass,
What I guessed while I lay alone in my bed . . . . and again as I
walked the beach under the paling stars of the morning.

My ties and ballasts leave me . . . . I travel . . . . I sail . . . . my elbows
rest in the sea-gaps,
I skirt the sierras . . . . my palms cover continents,
I am afoot with my vision. (63–64, 702–13)

In this last instance especially, where Whitman uses a "beauty of a stallion"
as a vehicle to, ultimately, blast his soul into the space of his "vision," the fusion is not just a matter of semantics. It is an instrument for this translation
of the language of the body into the language of the soul and vice versa. It

took me years to finally begin to see, and then more years to come to understand, what Whitman was making available to me: a way of thinking and talking about matters of the soul as something practical, useful, intrinsic to identity in all of its aspects; a way of thinking and talking that supersedes the more simplistic dualisms I was familiar with. That I missed it for so long is a good object lesson—for any number of things, I guess, not least of which is the value of coming back to re-read a poet of interest over and over until you're ready to get it.

Sometimes our relationships change dramatically, for better or worse, on the basis of the smallest of observations. That's what happened between me and Whitman the next time I came across this poem, in a graduate course in nineteenth-century American literature, reading all the routine stuff. Not much discussion in the class, not much life. So I'm reading the first "leaf" in the 1855 edition of *Leaves of Grass*, the poem that became "Song of Myself," kind of going through the graduate-school motions, and I come to the lines:

> Walt Whitman, an American, one of the roughs, a kosmos,
> Disorderly fleshy and sensual . . . . eating drinking and breeding,
> No sentimentalist . . . . no stander above men and women or apart
>   from them . . . . no more modest than immodest.
>
> Unscrew the locks from the doors!
> Unscrew the doors themselves from their jambs! (54, 498–503)

The line where he names himself is what stood out to me for some reason. I had always before heard that the same way I heard athletes or celebrities talk about themselves, arrogantly, in the third person. But, as it happened, quite luckily, this time we were, as I said, reading the 1855, the original, edition of the poem. That ragged, spectacular, raucous, unshapely, wash of words: the first incarnation of "Walt Whitman." I knew that his name, as author, was not on the book's frontispiece; that, in fact, the line I mention is the first time we can assign a name to the speaker of the poem. This time, I heard his self-naming not so much as a pronouncement of who the author was but as an announcement of who, henceforth, he had simply for his own hidden reasons decided, and wanted, to be. In effect, instead of seeing this as a gesture to assert a previously fixed identity, or even to create a new one, I saw it as an attempt to evade (which is a different thing altogether from Eliot's "escape") individual, local identity altogether—in formal terms, to use an epic "he" to free himself from the lyric "I," thereby, in the process creating an epic "I," without sacrificing one iota of the power of either, which I thought was both brilliant and amazing, this blowing the locks off doors and doors off their hinges. At that moment, I finally "got" Whitman, and I loved what I got. Here, I thought, is not some simplistic, pompous bully, Pound's pig-headed father, for example, leaving around huge chunks of wood because he's too lazy or stupid to hew them. No, here is someone so unique, so over the top, so brash and iconoclastic, that it wasn't even funny. Or was, in a good way. I remember when that thought crossed my mind that I actually laughed, the way I only do when, like the poem's doors, I'm just blown away by someone's brilliance, a habit that occasionally leads to misunderstanding ("he's laughing *at* me") and gets me into trouble. Fortunately, this new and improved Whitman was not that kind of guy. I just knew he would have the greatest sense of humor about himself—and about me. From that moment forward we have gotten along very amicably.

It is hard for us to fully appreciate the magnitude of Whitman's innovation in relation to this matter of poetic "identity." I generally think of the twentieth century, at least in terms of its poetics, as the century of the "image." But we could just as easily call it the "long poem" century, full of works that could never have taken their shapes without Whitman's as a model. There are the many episodic epics, like Pound's *Cantos,* for example, which depend entirely for their coherence on the epicized first person. Or the pastiche epics, like W. C. Williams's *Paterson,* where the figure of the "hero" is a strange amalgam of place, character, and poet. Or the too numerous to list long poems that emerged from the first- and second-generation projectivists, on the basic model of Charles Olson's *Maximus* poems. Or the many long, fervent poetic laments and rants like Allen Ginsberg's *Howl.* Even extended-series poems like John Berryman's *Dream Songs* or Robert Lowell's *History* or Anne Sexton's *Transformations* could not have been written as they were had not Whitman multiplied the possibilities for poetic structure, line, sequence, persona, and voice. So, as I said, we're pretty accustomed to permutations of the sort of thing Whitman was the first to find a way to do. But if you go back to Whitman's historical moment, it's a different stage and a different story. Remember the anecdote I told about my first lesson from the *Norton Anthology* in my sophomore year in college, the one involving the features of traditional Western epics? I don't recall the whole list now, but I know it was a short one, probably six or seven items. It included things like the larger-than-life hero, a descent into the underworld, pretty standard stuff. But underlying it all, clearly and inviolably, was the sharp divide between the epic hero and the poet/narrator who tells the story. So there is, first of all, no extant precedent for what Whitman does when he does it.

Moreover, Whitman is writing at the tail end of the age of the true lyric, the self-contained, inward-looking, private-emotion-based, personal poem that the Romantics were so expert at. Not ten years before Whitman penned *Leaves*, in 1846, Edgar Allan Poe wrote "The Philosophy of Composition," in which he examines the process that produced his famous poem "The Raven," the first poem I memorized *in toto,* back in the seventh grade. Here Poe famously sets the upper limit of his poem "at about one hundred lines," what could be realistically taken in "at one sitting" (2:261–62). He offers an essentially Aristotelian program for the production of such a poem: a single "vivid effect" to drive the poem, a rigorous script of formal and efficient elements to bring it into material being (2:260). For him, "a long poem is, in fact, merely a succession of brief ones—that is to say, of brief poetical effects" (2:261). Whitman, who can use a hundred lines to clear his throat, would beg to differ, and he offers all the evidence anyone would need to be fully persuaded in his *Leaves*.

Once I came to understand who this Walt Whitman was, whole sections of the poem started to shimmer with new identity-related possibilities. Whitman differentiates himself into a number of parts, for example, all orchestrated around and by this epic "I," as in this long passage, which attends to various binary versions of his "self:" the public and the private, the social and the personal, the inner and the outer, the body and soul:

> Trippers and askers surround me,
> People I meet . . . . the effect upon me of my early life . . . . of the
>   ward and city I live in . . . . of the nation,
> The latest news . . . . discoveries, inventions, societies . . . . authors old
>   and new,
> My dinner, dress, associates, looks, business, compliments, dues,
> The real or fancied indifference of some man or woman I love,
> The sickness of one of my folks—or of myself . . . . or ill-doing . . . .
>   or loss or lack of money . . . . or depressions or exaltations,
> They come to me days and nights and go from me again,
> But they are not the Me myself.
>
> Apart from the pulling and hauling stands what I am,
> Stands amused, complacent, compassionating, idle, unitary,

> Looks down, is erect, bends an arm on an impalpable certain rest,
> Looks with its sidecurved head curious what will come next,
> Both in and out of the game, and watching and wondering at it.
>
> Backward I see in my own days where I sweated through fog with
>   linguists and contenders,
> I have no mockings or arguments . . . . I witness and wait.
>
> I believe in you my soul . . . . the other I am must not abase itself to
>   you,
> And you must not be abased to the other. (31–32, 58–73)

Both in and out of the game: that's what becomes possible when "identity" is conceived primarily from the outside in, as a constitutive, epic force, rather than solely from the inside out, as an emotional singularity. And in such an economy, the soul does have quite a practical place for itself, and a role, not as the whole but as the other, and for the other, the lull that looses Whitman's "valved voice," which is not his, but yours (32, 77). Or mine. As he says:

> I resist anything better than my own diversity,
> And breathe the air and leave plenty after me,
> And am not stuck up, and am in my place. (46, 347–49)

Yes, this is, I now knew, not a "stuck up" man at all. He is in his place. He lets us be in our places, to think all of these thoughts that are never either entirely his or entirely ours, leaving plenty after him, so open, so tolerant, so generous, so diverse.

Just read the poem based on these assumptions about "identity," about the both riven and merged relationship between self and soul, and you'll see what I mean—everywhere. I've had the occasion, over the last decade or so, to teach this book, the 1855 edition of *Leaves of Grass*, three or four different times. At first reading, many students hate Whitman in exactly the way I did forty years ago, when I was about their age. I have no problem with that. "Apart from the pulling and hauling stands" what he is, "[b]oth in and out of the game, and watching and wondering at it." That's as good a place for a teacher to be as it is for a poet to be, whether he's over or under thirty. By the time we get done with the poem, most of these students end up liking him. Sometimes quite a lot. To help them get to that point, one of the places I go is the first three lines, the ones that disgusted me so completely when

I first heard them, especially the second line: "And what I assume you shall assume." The first few times I read that line, I thought of "assume" in its customary sense, as in one's assumptions, beliefs, principles: "By, God," I thought he was saying, "by the time we're done here you're going to think what I think. I'll make sure of that, even if I have to do it atom by atom." Now I hear that word in its much different sense, as a matter to taking things in, into one's soul, as they are, from the outside, of using not assertion to accumulate but openness to assimilate power and force. I assume Whitman. And he assumes me. In these lines he accords to me, to you, that power. We have the same access to the same universe via our own bodies and souls. His project here is not to get us to "know" him, or even his poem. These are mere vehicles he can use for showing us his celebration, and to inspire us to our own. In the poem's preface, he even invites us to do something like what I have done with his poem over the years: ". . . read these leaves in the open air every season of every year of your life, re-examine all you have been told at school or church or in any book, dismiss whatever insults your own soul, and your very flesh shall be a great poem and have the richest fluency not only in its words but in the silent lines of its lips and face and between the lashes of your eyes and in every motion and joint of your body . . ." (11–12). Simple as that. Do it. Do it now.

Whitman brings his poem to an ethereal, stuttering stop, closing this way:

> I too am not a bit tamed . . . I too am untranslatable.
> I sound my barbaric yawp over the roofs of the world.
>
> The last scud of day holds back for me.
> It flings my likeness after the rest and true as any on the shadowed
>   wilds.
> It coaxes me to the vapor and the dusk.
>
> I depart as air . . . I shake my white locks at the runaway sun,
> I effuse my flesh in eddies and drift it in lacy jags.
>
> I bequeath myself to the dirt to grow from the grass I love.
> If you want me again look for me under your bootsoles.
>
> You will hardly know who I am or what I mean,
> But I shall be good health to you nevertheless,
> And filter and fibre your blood.

> Failing to fetch me at first keep encouraged,
> Missing me one place search another,
> I stop somewhere waiting for you. (96, 1322–36)

Whitman was a fairly young man when he wrote this. All of this ecstatic dissolution, into the pure sound of a "barbaric yawp," into the "shadowed wilds," into the "vapor and the dusk" of the "last scud of day," into the "lacy jags" of the "runaway sun," and finally into the ubiquitous grass, well, such effusiveness is harder to muster as age advances and death takes on some of its grimmer guises, as it did for Whitman, for example, during the Civil War, when his work as a nurse engendered the sobering, somber *Drum Taps* poems and his grave, grief-laden elegy to Lincoln, "When Lilacs Last in the Dooryard Bloomed." All those war-lost souls are harder to bear than the one he imagines for himself a decade earlier, in "Song of Myself." But I give him a lot of credit for being able to arrange himself so graciously and to sing so tenaciously in the face of these (contrary) versions of the soul's ultimate demise. And he did it all after he was thirty, which I'm sure would have pleased that student in my first graduate seminar all those years ago.

Three ❦ World Enough, and Time

OR ABOUT FIVE OR SIX YEARS, I've been using the same format in my course description for freshman writing, with pretty good success. As I explain to the students, my ambition in the course is to introduce them to university-level intellectual work; to me, the two most important elements for facilitating such work are as follows:

1. You should be able to take a position of your own in relation to the assigned topic or material, one that you are committed to and are prepared to develop and explain. It will become clearer as the course goes on what I mean by a "position." But let me say at the outset that it is not a fixed opinion, belief, judgment, or already-established value that you feel compelled simply to declare and defend. It is more like a place you want to stand, with openness toward the ongoing negotiation that any good conversation makes possible, all of your inner resources at the ready, to be used,

as necessary, to continue the process of working out in detail, reflecting upon, and revising your original position.

2. You should be able not just to quote from but also to make use of the work of other writers. This sort of research takes some practice and involves careful and considered reading of your sources, as well as a strong sense of what your own position is. It is a way of acknowledging that your own position exists in the context of other publicly professed positions, upon which it depends, paradoxically, for its originality.

I often use Kenneth Burke's "unending conversation" metaphor to suggest to the students how such work takes place and why it is important for them to take their place in it:

> Imagine that you enter a parlor. You come late. When you arrive, others have long preceded you, and they are engaged in a heated discussion, a discussion too heated for them to pause and tell you exactly what it is about. In fact, the discussion had already begun long before any of them got there, so that no one present is qualified to retrace for you all the steps that had gone before. You listen for a while, until you decide that you have caught the tenor of the argument; then you put in your oar. Someone answers; you answer him; another comes to your defense; another aligns himself against you, to either the embarrassment or gratification of your opponent, depending upon the quality of your ally's assistance. However, the discussion is interminable. The hour grows late, you must depart. And you do depart, with the discussion still vigorously in progress. (110–11)

One common name for the most long-ongoing of these conversations is "tradition"—a term we use all the time both in and out of the academy and generally treat relatively unproblematically in relation to history, knowledge, and discourse. But whether one thinks in terms of process (the unending elaboration of the conversation) or its subsequent traces (the preservation of certain conversational elements in a sanctioned canon that readers can return to), one is fully ensconced in work that is intrinsically temporal, that takes one's own time and takes place in the context of long stretches of historical time that are not one's own, but can, in certain limited ways, be made so through reflexive reading.

✢

ROBERT BURNS DOES AS GOOD A JOB as anyone I've read at capturing the double affliction of temporality in the human condition. He talks here to the "wee, sleekit, cowran, tim'rous" mouse he has just dislodged, literally, from her nest with a plough:

> Still, thou art blest, compar'd wi' me!
> The present only toucheth thee:
> But Och! I backward cast my e'e,
> On prospects drear!
> An' forward, tho' I canna see,
> I guess an' fear! (*ERW* 213)

The mouse may have nothing much left at that moment, but her consciousness is at least confined to the blessed present, the now. Burns, on the other hand, like the rest of us, is almost always, by dint of his consciousness of time, somewhere else besides now. I agree with Burns that the mouse is better off in many respects. It's not so much the fact that, as humans, we have a built-in capacity to be aware of temporality in an extended way. To a certain degree, even the mouse has that. It's that we have complex, rich, deep connections, via memory and planning, to broad ranges of time that are not now. And it's those vast, empty spaces that end up being where we live a lot of our lives. Even that would be acceptable if only we also had the capacity to step outside of that framework from time to time. I've spent countless hours over the course of my life trying to gain some ground on the nature and meaning of my temporality. I have momentary glimmers of understanding—when, for example, I read people like Einstein or Heidegger or Coleridge or Augustine, among others, who seem to me to have some insight and clarity in this regard. But mostly I just get kind of vertiginous, as if prying myself away from the foundational nature of time leaves me with no points of reference to keep me steady. The primary symptom of this is a kind of "nausea" not unlike the one that Sartre's Roquentin feels, in the spatial dimension, as he looks at the tree and becomes cognizant of its being, its *mode* of being, as fundamentally alien to his.

A couple of months ago, before a meeting, I was talking with one of the teachers there about the weight of the past, specifically the fact that I tend to keep as few files and records as I can, almost nothing. My rule of thumb about documentary material is if it's not foreseeably reusable (teaching materials, say) or necessary for legal reasons (administrative records, say), I throw it out. Part of this has to do with my reclusive nature. But another part of it, I've been thinking recently, has a kind of "ecological" aspect, a desire to leave as little litter as I can for others to find along my way. I keep no student essays, no unfinished drafts of poems or articles, no correspondence, no duplicates of reports and spreadsheets. If you wanted to write my biography, you'd be hard pressed to find among my effects any trove of textual evidence to work with. In any case, I said to the teacher, "it just gives me the creeps to think about my own past," all that old, worn-out baggage to carry around, the evidentiary trail that time leaves for us, or that we create in a foolhardy and ultimately futile effort to stymie its inexorable passage—in the pictures we take, the papers we store, the "knowledge" we accumulate on shelves and in drawers, even, to some extent, in our recollections. It reminded me, I said, recalling a conversation I had had with my wife that morning, of the exoskeletons molted by cicadas that litter sidewalks by the thousands every seventeen years or so. Their carcasses look exactly like the real thing and are captivating to our attention for that reason. But you pick one up and it's just a flimsy, filmy, dried up, emptied out shell, perfectly lifeless—not dead, exactly; just a void utterly vacated by life. Creepy. And oddly mesmerizing.

I don't understand why we are so tempted to pick up, metaphorically, these sere carcasses to carry around with us, their weight growing incrementally greater as we age. That's how I think of the remnants of my past that distract and afflict me no matter how hard I try to hold them in abeyance. I want to do my best to resist those temptations, in part, at least, because, like Burns, what I see back there, when I have to look, are, quite often, a lot of "prospects drear." I don't mean to over-dramatize the difficulties of my personal past, or of our historical moment generally. Certainly I, we, live in a time of great luxury and leisure, at least by comparison to Burns's. And while I may, like Burns, sometimes cast a melancholy aspect over things I contemplate, I'm not talking about that either. What makes the past so "drear" is precisely its vacuity, what is absent from it: life. Going there is more like going to a funeral than to a wedding, a distinction to keep in mind in relation to Coleridge's mariner's choice of "the man that must hear me" (528, line 589).

I was for much of my life, on the other hand, quite captivated by the future, always looking ahead, planning, forecasting, leaping forward into that equally lifeless space where guesses have either paid off or not and fears are either realized or banished. It's a time, I know now, that never comes. I've spent some energy over the years trying to mitigate that set of temptations as well, to become what I think of as simply forward-looking, while still standing in the present, in the now. But ultimately, it's a Sisyphean task. The human condition is defined by temporality, forward and back, more than by any other force.

The reading process is a good vehicle for exposing this conundrum. First of all, to read a poem takes up *your* time: you must both remember and forecast equally and simultaneously, to persist in a moving present without getting so bogged down in the receding past that the process slows to a stop and without getting so entranced by the forthcoming future that the process short-circuits itself. Simultaneously, you must engage with the *poet's* time, historically to some extent, but more practically with the rhythms of time enacted in the text. And you must also engage with the *poem's* time, its narrative line. Beyond that, to read is, by definition, to assimilate productions from the past (what St. Augustine calls the not-now) as if they are approaching us from the future (what Augustine calls the not-yet), while inhabiting an impossibly evanescent present (that Augustine cannot seemingly account for or justify [191]). The word or sentence or book is an artifact of someone else's not-now, having been inscribed a millennium, a century, even a second ago. Yet it can come into existence only in our own not-yet, approaching us out of that futural mist.

The same can be said, in the broadest sense, about what we call the "tradition" within which academics, and most other professionals, operate intellectually. We use this word quite routinely, as if the transgressions of time it enacts were unproblematic. The tradition, we imagine, exists as an extant coherence. We argue over what belongs and what doesn't, about how things are more (or less) properly arranged, about hierarchies and values, as if those are the key problems. But, as a matter of fact, the constituent elements of any intellectual tradition are encoded primarily in its archivable texts, which exist, in their pastness, only as a disassembled smattering of lifeless artifacts. They precede us only in the most trivial of ways. For any reader, scholar or otherwise, interested in finding a way through, or a place inside of, the realm of a tradition, the material at hand exists only in our future, waiting to be intercepted as it approaches us, which is what happens when we read.

The re-reading process I describe in this book blurs even further the typical temporal sequence. No longer is the poet someone we can imagine as fixed, "dead," whose work can be thought of as finalized, either by its completion at some point in the past, slotted into its proper place in the schematic of a tradition, or now, in the reading, having been acquired as a body of knowledge. The re-reading process is circular, recursive, always both unfinished and unfinalizable; it covers the same ground over and over, each passage at a temporal remove from the preceding one but intimately contiguous with it, no matter how much actual time has passed in the interim. The text at issue belongs, to some extent, always to the future, moving up ahead, stopping from time to time, like Whitman promises to do at the end of "Song of Myself," to wait for us to catch up. And its place in the tradition is, therefore, always in a state of suspension, held in abeyance, open to negotiation and renegotiation. That is, to me, what makes it possible to think of long-dead poets as still at hand in an animate manner, "alive" as they approach us or we approach them, again and again, mired as we are in our own prospects drear, fraught as we are with our own guesses and fears.

The problem with time, then, is that while we are quite conscious of our place it, of its having passed and of its forthcomingness, we cannot stand in any position outside of it to get a real handle on it. It remains so endemic to our experience at the moment, and so encased in our recollections and anticipations, that, as Bakhtin said about telling one's own story, trying to think about it, and especially to write about it in any sort of a reflective way, is like trying to lift yourself up by your own hair. That's one of the reasons I admire thinkers like Bakhtin and Heidegger. They are simply better at thinking about time than I am. Or maybe they just have longer arms and stronger hair.

♣

"CLOSE READING," THE DOMINANT MODE of poetic reception when I started reading poets, favored a slowing down, even a radical slowing down, of readerly time. Poetry in particular, among all the discourses, according to this agenda, was to be scrutinized, savored, mulled, delved into. One would be encouraged, as it were, to circulate, gyre-like, in and among the verbal eddies of ambiguity, paradox, seeking ambitiously, assiduously, to get at the "hidden" meanings of the text. Time was nearly stilled by retarding the progression of one's attention through a text. Over and over. Slo-mo reading would have been a better term for it. But the "other method" I had already evolved for myself took me in the opposite direction, and I kept trying to maximize it, to speed up the reading process exponentially, to absorb, inhale, a whole page at once, a whole poem at once. I wondered what sort of stillness this might inspire if I could take it to the limit, to get the "experience" instantly, the way life happens? A deeply complex, almost electric one, I suspected. So I worked diligently to read poems faster and faster without losing focus, without skimming, trying to absorb each word as both a signal and a sound, but at the light-speed of sight. This discipline reached its apex for me when, as a junior in college, I sat down with the collected poetry of D. H. Lawrence, whom I had never read before. I started reading first at a normal pace, then pushed myself faster and faster until, by about the fiftieth page, I was reading a poem almost as fast as I could turn a page. The experience was exhilarating. The impact of each poem was like a hammer on my nervous system, emotion, thought, memory all flashing at once. I sensed each poem in a sort of instantaneously physical way, and then the next one and the next one, in a flood of perception that gave me the illusion at least that I was in some sort of exotic communion with Lawrence, that I not only "identified" with some of his experiences (which is fairly easy but simple) but actually saw the world from his shoes for a few extraordinary minutes (which is also fairly easy but more complex and interesting).

From then on, although I never was able to replicate the extremity of this particular reading experience, I was fully committed to what I started to call, to myself, by contrast with close reading, "far" reading. It seemed to me to be the difference between sitting on the moon and studying it bit by bit under a microscope, and standing on the earth and seeing it all at once through a telescope. These were fundamentally different ways of knowing, to be sure, each useful and productive and admirable. But the latter, this far reading, was radically new to me, unsanctioned, exciting to the utmost in every respect. I had the sense that time itself, as it was being meted out and measured by the necessarily metronomic character of language, was being cheated, worked around, defused, almost defeated: my present, the author's present—made consonant, the past and the future narrowed to a sharp focus on this binary moment. This intersection of two "positions" meant that all of those not-nows and not-yets were happening at once in one place.

This is one way of conceptualizing, and reflecting on, temporality on the minute scale of an individual reading experience. There are more extensive analogues: What, for example, should one make of the sort of repeated readings, over a lifetime, that are my subject in this book? Or, even more broadly, how does one account for the vast stretches of time that often separate acts of composition from acts of reception? These stretches of time are, in the case of the sort of poems I'm talking about here, canonical icons, colonized in so many different ways by critics and scholars who pile text upon gloss upon commentary on top of the original composition, building a sort of sedimented reef of material that needs to be if not dug through, then at least traversed. It is by means of this gradual accretion that canonical texts are, inevitably, pre-read for us, set into the tradition—even if the only symptom of that, for a seventh-grader, is the fact that someone has singled them out for inclusion in a cheap anthology.

✥

POETRY IS AMONG THE MOST time-managed modes of discourse, regimenting readers to its rigors on many different levels. There are all the superficial manifestations of this discipline: meter, rhyme, assonance, alliteration, and so on, the sorts of formal metrics we learn early on in school to recognize and identify. The kind of temporal matters I'm interested in here include these, but go much deeper. Lending oneself to a poet's "time" is, I believe, an essential element of engaging with the poet's "life." Time may sound like kind of an abstract, mechanical sort of thing. In poetry that's not the case at all. It's just the opposite. All those nights I spent reading poems in my bed as a teenager, well, I did it at least as much for physical as for intellectual pleasures: the cascading waves of sounds, the pulse of beats and rhymes, the deep feelings they elicited, these are bodily things, they are intimate, pleasurable rhythms we can ride into worlds unlike our own. When I read any new poet, one of my primary ambitions is to try on, really try on his or her "time," to walk around in it for a while, see how it re-organizes *my* experience, changes *my* world.

Ezra Pound's famous dictum, "An 'Image' is that which presents an intellectual and emotional complex in an instant of time" (96), first appeared in the same issue of *Poetry* as the imagist tenets I wrote about in chapter 1. Image was a term that had almost no currency in discussions of poetic technique in the nineteenth century. When it was used, it carried its most generic meaning. All of a sudden, during World War I, it became all the rage, and it remained one of the dominant concepts in poetics throughout the twentieth century. Why was that so? Part of the answer is that one of the taken-for-granted cultural conventions that got disrupted by the cataclysm of war, along with all the more obvious others, was simple temporal sequence—how one moment connected to the next—and this obviously affected the commonplaces of poetic time.

Poetry in the nineteenth century was regulated by, even differentiated from other literary genres by, standardized conventions of measure: meter, end-rhyme, stanzas, rhyming patterns. Individual poets could vary their poems quite a lot within such a system. But they all used these conventions almost all the time. Read almost any poet writing in the nineteenth century (Whitman and Stephen Crane are obvious exceptions I can think of offhand) and the work is measured by these metrics. Even on the prose side, the long, periodic sentences you get throughout the nineteenth century, sometimes a half page or more long, so challenging to navigate now, were made possible by certain assumptions about measured temporal progressions. In his essay "On Method," Coleridge differentiates methodized thinking (which he is recommending) from unmethodized thinking in precisely such terms:

> Both do, indeed, at once divide and announce the silent and otherwise indistinguishable lapse of time. But the man of methodical industry and honourable pursuits, does more: he realizes its ideal divisions, and gives a character and individuality to its moments. If the idle are described as killing time, he may be justly said to call it into life and moral being, while he makes it the distinct object not only of the consciousness, but of the conscience. . . . Of the good and faithful servant, whose energies, thus directed, are thus methodized, it is less truly affirmed, that He lives in time, than that Time lives in him. (*W* 449–50)

It is "control over time," "the METHOD of the will" (553), that makes possible the grand, flowing sentences, clause nested within clause, that were so commonplace in the work of Coleridge, Wordsworth, and their contemporaries. For them, the flow of time was unproblematically continuous and traditional metrics were the preferred way to parcel it out in poems. The modernists eschewed all of this not simply to indulge Pound's dictum to "make it new," but because they felt no such confidence in the untroubled flow of time. Theirs was a world of disruption, discontinuity, all the way down to the physical level: The publication of Albert Einstein's "On the Electrodynamics of Moving Bodies" in 1905 pronounced time officially "relative." So poets needed to find more pertinent modes of measurement to assert "control over time" in their poetic compositions, and they thought and argued a lot among themselves about what those should be. One of the terms of this debate that got a lot of traction is Pound's "instant."

A little bit later in "A Few Don'ts," Pound offers this advice to poets: "It is better to present one Image in a lifetime than to produce voluminous works" (97). Pound habitually offered his "In a Station of the Metro" as the exemplar for imagist compositions. Had Pound followed his own advice, his poetic career would have been over right then, in 1913. But he didn't, of course. He went on to write one of the most "voluminous works" of the twentieth century, his *Cantos,* an eight-hundred-page series of musical,

enigmatic poems written over a forty-year period, rife with Pound's iconoclastic views on twentieth-century poetics, politics, and "butchers." In order
to do that, he needed to figure out a way to put a lot of discontinuous "instants" together such that they were not discrete and separate poems, as did
all the other poets of his generation who started out as imagists: Eliot, Williams, H. D., to name an amazing few. They found many innovative ways to
solve this problem. Pound's rapid turn away from imagism—first to vorticism and then to futurism, both of which relied on dynamic conceptions of
time—over just a few years is one illustration of the urgency of this search.

A good entry point into the problem of sequencing instants is the third
tenet that F. S. Flint lists in "Imagisme": "As regarding rhythm: to compose
in the sequence of the musical phrase, not in sequence of a metronome" (95).
The metronome, which arbitrarily divides continuous time into pleasingly
equal beats, is an obvious reference to conventional poetic metrics. But what
does this musical phrase offer, in practical terms, as an alternative? Flint's
brief essay does not elaborate. But further on in "A Few Don'ts," among
some general comments about the musical properties of poetic rhythms,
Pound advises:

> Don't chop your stuff into separate *iambs*. Don't make each line
> stop dead at the end, and then begin every next line with a heave.
> Let the beginning of the next line catch the rise of the rhythm
> wave, unless you want a definite longish pause.
>
> In short, behave as a musician, a good musician, when dealing
> with that phase of your art which has exact parallels in music. The
> same laws govern, and you are bound by no others. (99–100)

Pound provides a long commentary on how he came to write "In a Station of the Metro," which he calls a "hokku-like sentence" (*V* 461) governed
by the laws of music rather than the "chop" and "stop" method. But what
interests me most is the difference between the metronome and the musical phrases as modes of poetic measurement. Take the last line of Pound's
poem: "Petals on a wet, black bough." You can scan it in traditional metrics,
most likely as a five-beat line, but what do you call the last three beats, which
to my ear are monosyllabic? You can start to mess around with spondees (a
foot with two long syllables) to do this. But the musical phrase makes all of
these complex machinations unnecessary. I realized as I was trying to write
about this poem that ever since I first read it, in college, I have heard that
line in my head as music, and I sing it to myself quite often. I can't read or
write music, so I can't represent what I hear in those terms. But my song

divides this line in five nearly equal measures: Petals / on a / wet/ black / bough. The tune varies by my mood, but the rhythm stays the same, and it actually *is* easier to think about it in musical terms.

Among subsequent poets, Louis Zukofsky made the most of this Poundian initiative; some of his poems (like his *Autobiography*) are actually scored musically in the text. Other poets dissented. William Carlos Williams, for example, did "not believe that writing is music," or that "writing would gain in quality or force by seeking to attain the conditions of music," primarily because he felt that music tempts (imaginatively liberated) words away from "natural objects" (*I*, 150). Williams preferred painting as a methodological analogue, and he goes on to invent the "variable foot" and "stepped triadic line" as his own instruments of measurement, with the ambition, again, of creating patterns of internal rhythm that are much more flexible, adaptable, and unpredictable than the metronomic foot and the end-stopped line. When you read a Williams poem, it is clearly lush with such patterns but very hard to parse with traditional metrics, and his experimentation evolved over the course of his career. With a couple of minor exceptions, the poems in *Spring and All* have lines beginning hard by the left-hand margin. By the 1940s, Williams's forms were much more fluid and responsive to their respective "instants." Look at these lines, for example, from book 2 of *Paterson*, the long epic he published in parts during the 1940s and 1950s.

> The descent beckons
>   as the ascent beckoned
>   Memory is a kind
> of accomplishment
>   a sort of renewal
>   even
> an initiation, since the spaces it opens are new
> places
>   inhabited by hordes
>   heretofore unrealized
> of new kinds— (77–78)

The triadic line and variable foot might seem like vague concepts in theory, but their effects on the management of time in these lines, or in so much twentieth-century poetry that borrowed his innovations, is immediately evident as embodied rhythm. Clearly Williams had one possible solution to the "instant of time" problem that imagism posed, relying more on models from the visual arts (painting and sculpture, especially) than from music to arrange his "things" in new rhythmic sequences.

The "instant" appears again as a primal unit of poetic measure almost forty years after Pound's dictum in the work of Charles Olson, who helped to found the Black Mountain school of poetry and coined the term "projectivism" to name another new method. Here is the last of the three "simplicities" that define the method, from his famous essay "PROJECTIVE VERSE," which appeared in 1950: "ONE PERCEPTION MUST IMMEDIATELY AND DIRECTLY LEAD TO A FURTHER PERCEPTION. It means exactly what it says, is a matter of, at all points . . . get on with it, keep moving, keep in, speed, the nerves, their speed, the perceptions, theirs, the acts, the split second acts, the whole business, keep it moving as fast as you can, citizen. And if you also set up as a poet, USE USE USE the process at all points, in any given poem always, always one perception must must must MOVE, INSTANTER, ON ANOTHER!" (17).

For Olson, a perception is much like a Poundian image, but in motion, always in motion toward another and another, which provides "the *kinetics* of the thing," the "energy," "instant by instant" of the poem's "FIELD" (16), the metaphor Olson borrowed from physics to convey the means by which individual, potentially static, images become dynamic in their relationships. Olson goes on to specify the "two halves" of the projective poem this way:

> The HEAD, by way of the EAR, to the SYLLABLE
> The HEART, by way of the BREATH, to the LINE (19)

It was the second line of this tandem, which I'll talk about below, that had the most immediate influence on poetic measurement, especially during the 1970s when the breath-paced line became a commonplace in the economy of poetic methods. But the first line is actually more radical in its ambition to reconfigure the relationship between measure and meaning, or in the more familiar terms of modernist poetics, which the projectivists picked up, between form and content.

Olson's identification of the syllable as the fulcrum for poetic meaning makes time a full semantic component of the poem's process. For Olson, the "smallest particle" of a poem's time is not the traditional foot, nor is the smallest particle of the poem's meaning the word. In both cases, it is the syllable, which thereby, for him, establishes it at the poem's intellectual core. Compare the following statement by Olson about the relationship between mind and time to the one I quoted from Coleridge about method: "Consider

the best minds you know in this here business: where does the head show, is
it not, precise, here, in the swift currents of the syllable? can't you tell a brain
when you see what it does, just there? . . . So, is it not the PLAY of a mind we
are after, is not that that shows whether a mind is there at all?" (19).

For Coleridge, the "control over time" operates globally over a whole
text and its ambition is toward synthesis and, ultimately, closure; for Olson,
such control operates syllable by syllable, "instant by instant" (16), throughout the poem, which achieves coherence only as an aggregate, chronically
"in the open," available for infinite extension (148). This is a fundamentally
different way of conceptualizing the mind in its temporal relations, via language, to meaning, and it is easy to see why so many of the projectivist long
poems remained "unfinished:" A terminus in such a field will always be
temporally arbitrary. Interestingly though, for both Coleridge and Olson,
the meticulous management of time is an index of intelligence, of the mind
at work (Coleridge) or play (Olson.)

The "threshing floor for the dance" of intellect is "the LINE" (19), which
for Olson is controlled by the poet's breath. This is a further departure from
traditional measures than music, which has universal properties. The breath
is individual, unique to a poet, an embodiment of the poem's specific moment, of the poet himself, in his intimate relationship with us also, as we
adapt our own breathing to the lines on the page:

> And the line comes (I swear it) from the breath, from the breathing
> of the man who writes, at the moment that he writes . . .
>   Because breath allows *all* the speech-force of language back in
> . . . because, now a poem has, by speech, solidity, everything in it
> can now be treated as solids, objects, things . . . (19–21)

As is the case with Williams's variable foot and triadic line, there is no
simple, one-to-one correspondence between concept and effect. The tre-
mendous range of difference among projectivist poets—the sweep of Robert Duncan, the clipped precision of Robert Creeley, the sensuous intensity
of Denise Levertov—is one index of this potential for multiplicity, made
possible by uniquely individuated breath-based lines. On the reader's side,
the method requires a more intense focus on the "speech-force of language"
than is required, for example, by more traditional poets. Until you actually
catch the eccentric measures of a specific poet's speech-time, which cannot
be separated out from the semantic element of the poem (and codified in
abstract terms, as traditional metrics can), then the poems resist entrance.

Olson, for example, like Whitman, is "large" and contains "multitudes," which are congregated in his multivolume masterpiece *The Maximus Poems* under the rubric of his epic-hero Maximus, whose name alone conveys Olson's preferred proportions. So the best way to catch his breath, with all the permutations and variations that his specific syllable/breath calculus can engender, is in big doses. Robert Creeley, at the other extreme, can be sipped and savored in much smaller samples. These two poets are formally quite different, but when read with breath-pacing as the main regulator, the ways time affects meaning—along with Creeley's mantra that "FORM IS NEVER MORE THAN AN EXTENSION OF CONTENT" (qtd. in Olson 16)—become almost physically self-evident.

The Maximus Poems served as a prototype for the plethora of "long poems" that poured forth from second-generation projectivists in the 1970s and 1980s, and one can see why: Olson came up with a very good method for orchestrating "instants" into long organic arrangements. His poem moves like a fast-forward staccato sequence of brightly illuminated flash-photos with hardly a breath-space between one and the next. Once you catch the pace, it's exciting, almost a sensory overload. Olson's method became more and more mercurial as his epic progressed over the years he worked on it. The first few volumes look and feel like a hybrid of Pound's *Cantos* and Williams's *Paterson*. Thereafter, Olson was more experimental both in terms of the poems' objectivity—he preferred the term "objectism," to evade entirely the binary relationship with "subjectivity," with which "[i]t is now too late to be bothered" (24)—and its visual cadences. There are, for example, lines glancing off at odd angles on the page, or lines askance from one another connected by arrows, or lines that have their primary locus of meaning at the level of syllable and sound. These later volumes are breath-challenging in their arrangements, ranging from pages dense and packed with left-hugging lines to full 8x11 (parchment quality in the original edition) pages, with just three or four cryptic words. Such projectivist innovations provided an impetus for many kinds of experimentations in the 1960s and 1970s, from the short-lived fascination with "concrete" poems, some of which were rendered in the shape of the subject of the poem, a flower for example, to more language-based movements.

One of the most interesting and enduring among the latter were what came to be called the L=A=N=G=U=A=G=E poets (after the title of journal edited by Charles Bernstein and Bruce Andrews, the East Coast node of the movement). It is not possible to pin down a single, specific identity for this movement, which had so many off-centers, rifts, and manifestos. You need

to read the poets—you can identify a dozen easily with a keyword search—
for yourself to see the variety of things the poets are trying to do with time,
and how. Larry Eigner, who along with Barrett Watten anchored the West
Coast node of the movement, is one of my favorites. Here is a passage from
his work during the 1970s:

> D A N G E R I N T H A T , T O O
>
> Time and again, different, the same
> the houses,   snow or / and the trees
> fire   signs put at the distance
> (bricks and slick chimney
>
> > time
>
> one place to another, and
> the present always is here
> well a different concern (139)

Eigner's poems, like those of many of the Language poets, are timed both
line by line and within the lines in quite rigorous ways. And they explore the
evocative intersections of words as/and things that so appealed to Williams
as elements of the "American idiom." These are clearly not the rhythms
of Wordsworth or even of Whitman. There may be traces of Williams's
stepped lines and gestures to Olson's unusual use of punctuation marks to
regulate timing. But they are new rhythms, pertinent to their moment, new
ways of keeping time, of living in and into instant upon instant, as the poet
processes and presents them for us.

THE 1920S WERE THE HEYDAY, from my point of view, of space-time thinking. Einstein won the Nobel Prize in physics in 1921. He was a celebrity.
The concept of relativity was reaching the popular imagination and many
of its implications and potentials were starting to be worked out. Quan-
tum mechanics was just beginning to offer an ever more radical picture
of space-time at the atomic level. The impact of all this was felt as well
in philosophy and poetics, which are more the domain of my inquiry. I
want to consider three figures whose work in that regard originated in this
cultural/intellectual hotbox: T. S. Eliot and Martin Heidegger, and, most
especially, Mikhail Bakhtin, who was writing his first major book, on Dos-
toevsky's poetics, around this time. I want to translate some of Bakhtin's
concepts—dialogue and the chronotope, primarily—and certain aspects of

his method—his general ambition to see literature as a vehicle for embodying human experience and human wisdom and the activity of reading as inherently, and potentially transformatively, ethical—over to my re-readings of the poets that interest me, to flesh out a scholarly framework for the "life of the author" part of my argument.

In "Discourse in the Novel," his most famous and widely read essay, Bakhtin marks a sharp distinction between poetic discourse and novelistic discourse. The former (poetic), is a mode of single-voiced or "monologic" discourse (280) and by dint of its inherently (generically determined) "unitary and indisputable" (286) character, is precluded from the double-voiced dynamism that animates the latter (novelistic), which, as a mode of "dialogic," discourse (273), "reveals . . . the socially heteroglot multiplicity of its names, definitions and value judgments" (278). Novels, in other words, for Bakhtin at least, are better than poetry for representing "life." Certainly, in the framework of modernist critical systems and the diverse array of formalisms that emerged in Bakhtin's Russia around the same time, such a distinction is compelling. And postmodernism does little, I believe, to call it into serious question.

In my earliest readings of poets, I did in fact construe their "voices" as unitary and authoritative in precisely the ways that Bakhtin attributes these (limiting) qualities to poetic discourse. Part of this was a function of the way I happened to think about the role and status of poetry as a genre; another part was a function of the fact that first readings have this tendency by their nature, as we seek to organize our response to a particular poet, preliminarily, in manageable terms. The biggest part, though, is the fact that I was compelled to position myself, due to a variety of very clear (in retrospect) autobiographical, historical, and cultural forces, as an adamantly unitary and authoritative readerly presence. I consider this, now, as part of my good fortune, in that I felt perfectly qualified, fully competent, to engage with these poets as an equal and as much on my own terms as on theirs. I could, in other words, imagine myself as having a collegial conversation, rather than listening to a lecture. But the process of repeated, subsequent readings, as I have been trying to document here, serves gradually to dismantle, via its inevitable complications and interrogations, such a pristine binary partnership, introducing a range of what I believe can legitimately be called Bakhtinian heteroglossia—"a special type of *double-voiced discourse*" (324)—not least of which is the simultaneous presence of the multiple, sometimes mutually contradictory but equally competent, authoritative readings that we inherit as part of our cultural tradition. Beyond that, as my own historical record demonstrates, the authors themselves have over the years grown more and more dis-unified to my way of understanding.

I like Bakhtin for a lot of reasons. One of them is the seemingly mutually contradictory effects he has on my readerly "understanding." I feel in the first take on his work that I am baffled, flailing about, failing to get what he has to offer. But when I sit down to write about him, as I do here, taking him passage by passage to organize and support an argument, he seems quite lucid. What I hear is not always what other critics hear. But in some respects this paradox is simply another illustration of the sort of relationship I have been talking about. To a large extent, over time, through chronic dialogue with an author, we come to terms with one another. It's not so much either his yielding to me or my yielding to him. It's a relationship, one we negotiate and renegotiate, toward mutual understanding, often through a third text, like this one, which is neither entirely mine nor Bakhtin's. I borrow his voice and replace it with mine, by which means it becomes this third voice. This is not, again, the exact meaning of what he called "double-voicedness," but I'll call it that anyway. Actually, it's more like the kind of intellectual ventriloquism that allows us to "make use of" the parts of the ongoing Burkean conversation that help us to speak up for ourselves.

One of the terms I had in mind when I first started reading poets was, in fact, "dialogue," in its more mundane, everyday sense, as a conversation; and I believed I was entering into one with each of these authors as a careful listener and confident respondent. I imagined dialogue to be the reason they had written these things in the first place—the hope that someone they could have no way of prefiguring would talk back to them with engagement, tension, and urgency. Certainly that's what I imagined a writerly career would be like when I projected one potentially before me. Though I knew I would be absent from the conversations that might take place around my own works, I felt encouraged at the thought that at least there would be a conversation going on of the sort that I was quite often (though not always) incapable of initiating or sustaining among my local circle of peers.

So the first term I want to borrow from Bakhtin is "dialogue," as he uses it in a passage like this one: "The word in living conversation is directly, blatantly, oriented toward a future answer-word: it provokes an answer, anticipates it and structures itself in the answer's direction. Forming itself in an atmosphere of the already spoken, the word is at the same time determined by that which has not yet been said but which is needed and in fact anticipated by the answering word. Such is the situation of any living dialogue" (280). A "living conversation" is almost exactly what I felt was happening when I started to read poets. Whatever differences of time and place might intervene, the connection, I felt, was intimate, "close" in a way that is entirely different from the sense in which that term was being used in the dominant critical lexicon.

For Bakhtin, "[r]esponsive understanding is a fundamental force, one that participates in the formulation of discourse, and it is moreover an *active* understanding, one that discourse senses as resistance or support enriching the discourse" (280–81). I especially like this term "responsive understanding," which suggests to me that the "active" aspect of this process—"resistance or support"—takes place on both sides of the equation, with an author who orients his discourse toward me and with me who orients my engagement, through his discourse, toward him. As Bakhtin explains: "It is precisely such an understanding that the speaker counts on. . . . The speaker breaks through the alien conceptual horizon of the listener, constructs his own utterance on alien territory, against his, the listener's, apperceptive background" (282). This is the "new form of internal dialogism" that Bakhtin lays out (282). And one of the primary instruments for its implementation is what he calls the "chronotope," which is how I get back here, now, to the theme of time.

Bakhtin uses the concept of the chronotope—which he picked up in 1925 from a lecture by A. A. Uxtomskij on the use of chronotopes in biology—to help him describe the dynamic interrelationship of these various word-worlds—the ones belonging to the author and his own time, to the reader and his own time, to the story and its own time, to the story's characters and their own times—in the activity of reading. He defines his (literary) version of this space-time nexus this way, pretty straightforwardly (for him): "We will give the name *chronotope* (literally, 'time space') to the intrinsic connectedness of temporal and spatial relationships that are artistically expressed in literature. This term [space time] is employed in mathematics, and was introduced as part of Einstein's Theory of Relativity. . . [W]e are borrowing it for literary criticism almost as a metaphor (almost but not entirely). What counts for us is the fact that it expresses the inseparability of space and time" (84). And then, in the last section of the same essay, he comes at it again in this denser and more complex form: "Thus the chronotope, functioning as the primary means for materializing time in space, emerges as a center for concretizing representation, as a force giving body to the entire novel. All the novel's abstract elements—philosophical and social generalizations, ideas, analyses of cause and effect—gravitate toward the chronotope and through it take on flesh and blood, permitting the imaging power of art to do its work" (250).

Bakhtin wrote most of his essay on chronotopes, "Forms of Time and Chronotopes in the Novel," in the 1930s, while the New Criticism was being transported to America via the Southern Agrarians. The final section, "Concluding Remarks," from which the second definitional passage above comes, he added in 1973, when the essay was first published in Russia. This was two years before he died and just after I started graduate school. The English translation of this essay, in *The Dialogic Imagination*, did not appear until 1981, when I got my first tenure-track position. This sense of collapsing time, two generations of time, into one artifactual entity is, to me, a dramatic enactment of chronotopicity.

The bulk of the essay, written mostly when Bakhtin was in his late thirties, is primarily a taxonomic catalogue of an array of standard Western "novelistic" chronotopes from the early Greek modes of adventure writing to the raucous, ribald, carnivalistic style of Rabelais, with a smattering of more recent examples of their re-application. The much-later-appended conclusion, on the other hand, is sweepingly theoretical and stunningly insightful. It is as if, having spoken at great length, Bakhtin stopped for a forty-year moment to clear his throat (or fill his head) and, on the basis of that intervening reflection, which is invisible to us, told us exactly what it was good for—all of that history carried into the text via the simple footnote attached at the very end of the essay: "The 'Concluding Remarks' were written in 1973" (258). It is really impossible to read this essay through the retrospective lens of that footnote without having in mind, to some extent, not just the deeply moving accomplishments, trials, and travails of Bakhtin's biography, even if it's only the fragmentary version that I have accumulated incidentally over the years, but also the history of Russian Communism, the rise of the Soviet empire, the Cold War, the gulags, the combination of which prevented one of the most original minds of the century from finding a worldwide audience until after his death—all compressed into the second it takes us to read through the space between the essay's penultimate and final sections. Through the chronotopic impact of that footnote, this author is brought back to life in all of the ways he would consider, as I do, appropriate and useful.

It's this concluding section of this text—much more radical and synthetic theoretically than what precedes it—that really gets me where I want to go in terms of authorial "life." He opens the section, for example, this way: "A literary work's artistic unity in relationship to an actual reality is defined by its chronotope. . . . Abstract thought can, of course, think time and space as separate entities and conceive them as things apart from the emotions and values that attach to them. But *living* artistic perception . . . makes no such divisions and permits no such segmentation. It seizes on the chronotope in all its wholeness and fullness" (243).

The connection between art and "life" is now in place, expressed directly and authoritatively: a relationship between "[a] literary work's artistic unity" and "actual reality" that is orchestrated by the chronotope.

Through the chronotope, "[t]ime becomes, in effect, palpable and visible; the chronotope makes narrative events concrete, makes them take on flesh, causes blood to flow in their veins" (250). Time is fully integrated with the flesh and blood life-force of the discourse. Bakhtin then dramatically generalizes the scope of the chronotope, as a built-in feature of language and, even, the word itself: "Language, as a treasure-house of images, is fundamentally chronotopic. Also chronotopic is the internal form of a word, that is, the mediating marker with whose help the root meanings of spatial categories are carried over into temporal relationships (in the broadest sense)" (251).

And finally (for my purposes) Bakhtin uses the concept of the chronotope to integrate both author and reader as active and interactive components of "the work as a whole" (252):

> The text as such never appears [to the reader] as a dead thing; beginning with any text . . . we always arrive . . . at the human voice, which is to say we come up against the human being. . . . In the completely real-life time-space where the work resonates, where we find the inscription or the book, we find as well a real person—one who originates spoken speech as well as the inscription and the book—and real people who are hearing and reading the text . . .
>
> The work and the world represented in it enter the real world and enrich it, and the real world enters the work and its world as part of the process of its creation, as well as part of its subsequent life, in a continual renewing of the work through the creative perception of listeners and readers. (252–54)

All of the elements that interest me are now in play, as legitimate and profoundly dynamic aspects of the reading process, orchestrated dialogically via multiple chronotopes: the inner spatiotemporal structure of the narrative; the relationship between the represented world and an actual world; the author *qua* author performing his professional work in the context of the pertinent tradition; the real life-world of the author; the reader in the active process of re-animating the proffered text, often in the conscious context of mastered traditions; the reader as a real living organism whose "life" will be impacted by this process, which is profoundly social in all of its aspects and implications. This is an ideal method for re-reading poets.

❧

I TURN NOW TO THAT WIDER, deeper aspect of "time," the long haul, which we view through the refracting lens of what we call "tradition," particularly as it pertains to the ways we engage with historically remote poetic texts and their now-dead authors. This process is considerably more problematic than our most customary modes of reading, as well as our pedagogies, seem to presume. One problem we encounter as we face the text, which awaits our approach, is how to navigate across the expanse of time that separates the author who seeks to speak and we who seek to speak back. How is it possible to engage in a meaningful dialogue with an interlocutor who is not only spatially absent (a readerly problem that has both afflicted and preoccupied Western philosophy and criticism at least since Plato) but temporally remote (a readerly problem our culture has approached much more ham-handedly)? And then how do we fit what we find into the larger matrix of related texts?

No one acquires a discursive or disciplinary tradition in the temporal sequence in which it was produced. A philosopher, for example, does not begin his reading with Heraclitus and then follow the timeline up through history, reading every single extant philosophical text up to say, Žižek, noting along the way, in textbook fashion, the sequential progression that is taking place. No, the tradition precedes our reading, like a pre-assembled frame with marked places to install canonical texts once we've processed them; or a sort of formatted screen upon which we can bring up the various texts we actually do have time to read in a piecemeal or ornamental way, as if they are decorative accomplishments.

A few weeks ago I was at an event at which my son was receiving an award for an essay he wrote on Louis Armstrong for Black History Month. One of the odd and interesting things about being a parent is that you quite often find yourself in places or at occasions that you would otherwise not even know existed, let alone seek out. When my kids were younger and I was still in training as a parent (and human being, to some extent) I had a hard time with events of this sort. You spend two or three hours crowded into a cramped school auditorium basically to witness the few minutes that your own kid sings in the back row of a chorus. I'm not by nature a patient person. To the extent that I've become better at that, it has been through conscious labor, and situations of this kind have been helpful in that regard. As much for my own survival as for any more broadly spiritual reasons, I gradually came to appreciate these experiences precisely because I would never on my own have sought them out. It felt like I was being plucked out of my own personal history and plopped down in another one, one I would have no way to imagine by myself. This alternate history began to seem both strange and exotic to me, very engaging, an opportunity to, in effect, have an unexpected and potentially adventuresome side trip, one full of surprises, if only because I had no initiative of personal desire to frame a coherent set of expectations. Now I actually enjoy these little unplanned vacations to which I can "escape" by reveling in their spectacle. The distinction I have evolved for myself to help me in my progress away from irritation and toward revelry involves two ways of "attending." In the first, one attends (as in goes to) because one must, as a mode of endurance, a suspension of life until the interlude is over. In the second one attends (as in focuses) in the moment as a mode of living fully in and through its interim. The second is much better.

For this event, I had no idea what to expect going in, but it turned out to be a very large, important, and well-orchestrated ceremony with a long local history, all of which impressed me. It also had certain odd aspects that I found engaging to my "attention." One had to do with its dramatically biracial aspect. The contest was sponsored by a large local bank, represented at the event by an amiable and competent-sounding white vice president; it was promoted by a local mainstream rock radio station, represented by a ditzy, over-animated, young, white, female radio personality; the main speaker was a recently retired African American symphony musician, a deep, quiet, eloquent, profoundly moving ethical presence; the audience was split about evenly by race, as were the contest winners. It was a strange and kind of vaguely discomfiting mix. But I found myself, as I said above, reveling quietly (if that's possible) in its uniquenesses. When it came time for my son to receive his award, I picked up the small video camera we have for such moments. The moment I raised it up to frame the shot, I lost my connection to the moment and, instantly, became irritated. I'm sure this has happened to me many times before in such situations, but this time I was intensely conscious of it, very unhappy about it, and quite aware of the fact that the change was effected primarily by the camera. So I've been thinking about this lately.

As I said earlier, I have a temperamental aversion to the past and, as a consequence, I don't much like to take and almost never look at "old" pictures. The whole process of taking, storing, and occasionally disgorging them for collective viewing is torturous to me. What struck me in this situation, though, was the even more alienating effect of having to view the scene being recorded on a LCD viewing screen rather than through a glass viewfinder. As soon as I had to look at the screen instead of at my son walking up for the award I felt like I had been transported out of the time I was in and into some other remote, disconnected time, not quite the future, in which I would, perhaps, be viewing the video I was in the process of recording, but a sort of hyper-time, in both senses of the word: above and outside of "the present" and producing an unpleasant, jittery anxiety, as if I had drunk too much espresso. These two qualities (being both apart from and moving too fast through an experience) force a disjunction between immediate space-time, what's right in front of one at the moment, and what's on the screen; between one's immediate visual proprioception and one's visual-processing "memory." This temporal short-circuit creates a very unnerving (literally) kind of confusion. At that moment, I became aware of it and didn't like it.

I bring all of this up because I believe this experience can serve as an effective analogy for some of the most deleterious effects of the "tradition" on how we learn to read "great books," the canon. The following passages frame out the problem in a provocative way. They were both written in rough historical proximity to Bakhtin's listening to Uxtomskij talk about the use of chronotopes in biology, setting the seeds for his own work on chronotopes in Western narrative history. That was 1925. T. S. Eliot's essay "Tradition and the Individual Talent" was first published in 1920. In it, he writes:

> Tradition is a matter of much wider significance. It cannot be inherited, and if you want it you must obtain it by great labour. It involves, in the first place, the historical sense . . . ; and the historical sense involves a perception, not only of the pastness of the past, but of its presence. . . . This historical sense, which is a sense of the timeless as well as of the temporal and of the timeless and of the temporal together, is what makes a writer traditional. And it is at the same time what makes a writer most acutely conscious of his place in time, of his contemporaneity. (*SW* 49)

Martin Heidegger's *Being and Time* came out in 1927, which was just around the time I. A. Richards started handing out poems without authorial attribution, another way of manipulating temporality, by de-historicizing the artifact. Heidegger writes:

> When tradition thus becomes master, it does so in such a way that what it 'transmits' is made so inaccessible . . . that it rather becomes concealed. Tradition takes what has come down to us and delivers it over to self-evidence; it blocks our access to those primordial 'sources' from which the categories and concepts handed down to us have been in part quite genuinely drawn. Indeed it makes us forget that they have had such an origin, and makes us suppose that the necessity of going back to these sources is something we need not even understand. . . . Consequently, . . . Dasein no longer understands the most elementary conditions which would alone enable it to go back to the past in a positive manner and make it productively its own. (*BT* 43)

So all of these very smart men are thinking about temporality and the human condition at about the same time. I want to make a few comments on the concept of, and effects of, tradition on our customary modes of reading "great" books, based on the two quite distinct conceptions of tradition that are presented by Eliot and Heidegger, not so much for their own sake, but primarily to set up the subsequent, extensive, and more practical analysis of a poem by Parmenides that I've been thinking about for many years and that, as it happens, allows me to make exactly the point I want to make about the LCD-screen of tradition and its effect on our reception of important works.

Jonathan Ree, in talking about Heidegger's sense of the potential value of "tradition" for sustained intellectual work in his own discipline, philosophy, observes: "Inheriting a tradition is not the same as commemorating it; indeed, it is rather the opposite. You come into possession of an inheritance by taking it over and giving it a new opening on to the future, not by tagging along behind it and taking your orientation from the past" (13). Commemoration and inheritance are not terms that Heidegger relies on persistently as dominant concepts in *Being and Time*. Certainly in his much later *Discourse on Thinking* he is expressly concerned with the potentially disabling (for both artist and audience) effects of superficial commemoration. He says, in a speech he was making in his own home town to celebrate the 175th birthday of the musical composer Conradin Kreutzer, the type of occasion that is fraught with all of the potentially disabling effects of "commemorative" thinking: "For nowadays we take in everything in the quickest and cheapest way, only to forget it just as quickly, instantly. Thus one gathering follows on the heels of another. Commemorative celebrations grow poorer and poorer in thought. Commemoration and thoughtlessness are found side by side" (*DT* 45).

I want to borrow Heidegger's frustration with "commemoration" as a bridge between the story about my son's event and some of the problems with stereotypical modes of reading poets. My experience at the event is a small illustration of the loss of "there-being"—a Heideggerian concept (*Dasein*) that means more than I'm making of it in this instance—that can result when one seeks to still a moment so that it can be archived in perpetuity. It's a long way from this to a broad critique of the way poetry tends to get taught in school, but, really, you don't have to think about it long and hard to see how so much pedagogy is driven primarily by a desire to commemorate. Many of the critical strategies and testing methods we (as students) were and are trained with have the effect (though it is not inevitable that they should) of dissociating us from any real engagement with the material we are studying.

Whether "inheritance" offers the most effective counter to commemoration is arguable, as Eliot and Heidegger illustrate with their differing takes on its nature and its merits. Both of them, I think, are imagining the sort of inheritance that the tradition represents as a kind of potential wealth. Eliot, perhaps because of his American roots and our innate aversion to purely class-based rather than "labour"-produced legacy, tends to see inheritance as, really, just another mode of commemoration. We blithely assimilate the great books in whatever pre-existing framework is provided. For Eliot, no good writing can emerge from such a passive attitude toward what came before, nor can any full and sustained reading of a significant work emerge on its basis. His point is well taken. One could argue that especially in "Tradition and the Individual Talent," from which I quote above, he is more interested in the readerly work of the aspiring *writer*, which he is; but both here and elsewhere he makes quite clear that any reader of poetry who purports to be serious needs to achieve the same kind of command over the tradition as the writers he wants, seriously, to read.

Aside from the obvious elitism of Eliot's attitude and program, which has always rubbed me the wrong way, the main problem with this way of imagining the vitality of the tradition is that its inherent temporality seems always—despite the appearance of balance—to be striving toward time-lessness—everything potentially co-existent in a transcendent stasis. This would not be too bad, but the integrity of the "life" that produces the work is simultaneously vitiated, to be dismembered and reassembled in whatever "objective correlative" the poet decides to compile. To a certain degree, I'd say, the reader of the poem is similarly dismembered. This "stillness" may resemble peace, but it feels more to me like an unnerving effacement of our innately temporal natures that promotes his famous ambition to "escape from personality" (*SW* 56), or even the "continual extinction of personality" (52), which is of a different and scarier order of magnitude.

Heidegger, on the other hand, sees inheritance not as a legacy handed down from the past but as a possibility that approaches from the future. This sense of the value of the past is more European, the presence all around of extensive historical depth, of the resources of knowledge not just available in archival ways but built into the language and the culture, already part of the "there" of one's "being." One must work hard to extract the possibilities of an inheritance from the concealment of a tradition that makes it "inaccessible" by handing it down as self-evident, which it decidedly is not. One must come to understand it on one's own terms, with full respect for its "sources," in something like the same way, I would say, that I try to encourage my freshman writers to engage with their sources from the context of their own positions. This process, I would say, is neither mysterious nor available only to great philosophers. It's a very practical matter of considering how and why one engages with sources in the first place.

Heidegger offers any number of metaphors to promote an active sense of inheritance. In *Being and Time* he delineates aspects of his hermeneutic through terms like "uncovering" (227) and "care" (235) and even "understanding" (182, 385). In *Discourse on Thinking* he uses the metaphor of "rootedness" (48) toward the same end. And he recommends a mode of thinking he calls "meditative" (47), which he contrasts with the inherently superficial and destructive kind of thinking, called "calculative" (46), that dominates and diminishes the modern world. But the key point I want to make is that tradition, as it is handed down to us in its most convenient and conventional forms—as digested "categories and concepts," for example, the sort of thing that textbooks are particularly good at—is fundamentally a hindrance to understanding. It "uproots" rather than grounds us, disabling our ability "to go back to the past in a positive manner and make it productively [our] own" (43).

So how is it, then, that one *does* make the past productively one's own? Heidegger devotes most of the last third of *Being and Time* to this part of his project. More lucidly, he demonstrates a very assiduous and rigorous *poetic* method of reading in later works like *Early Greek Thinking* (where he primarily tackles Heraclitus) and *On the Way to Language* (where he primarily tackles Stefan George, Georg Trakl, and Friedrich Holderlin). The method I'm writing about in this book is quite a bit different from his. But it has one thing in common: Making the past productively our own requires not that we "escape from personality"—either our own or the poet's—but that we find ways to evade the most deceptive and debilitating screens through which the tradition is filtered forward to us, at various degrees of pixelization, and go back "to those primordial 'sources'" to meet them personally and directly.

♣

I HAVE BEEN ENGAGED WITH Parmenides, the Greek thinker, Socrates' teacher, for about forty years, more recently with growing interest. This history provides a good object lesson concerning the re-reading process and the distracting and irritating effects of the many sorts of screens through which we "inherit" the tradition. Parmenides may seem an odd choice in an argument of this sort: why a philosopher rather than a poet? The interesting thing about Parmenides and the other pre-Socratics, like Empedocles and Heraclitus, is that their actual work, though it has been claimed by and absorbed into the *philosophical* tradition, eludes any easy generic categorization. When you actually read the texts, it is hard to place them clearly in any specific disciplinary category. They are religion, philosophy, science, myth. But most of all, they read like poetry. It took me many years to realize that and to read the texts that way, primarily as poetry, I mean. But that is what makes Parmenides an ideal example for this illustration.

Parmenides wrote just prior to the age of Pericles, that high point of Greek culture, at which time, among other things, disciplinary thinking began to take over. We can see evidence of this over and over in the Platonic dialogues. When Socrates argues with Protagoras and Gorgias, for example, about the vacuity of sophistic rhetoric, it is almost always by contrast with disciplinary alternatives with proprietary "content." And by the time we get to Aristotle, poetics and rhetoric—not to mention physics, meteorology, metaphysics, ethics, and politics—are sharply differentiated from one another, with each consigned to its own separate book. But read Parmenides—or any of the other pre-Socratics for that matter—and, as I said, human knowledge seems all of a piece rather than a pre-sliced, multidisciplinary pie.

While it is impossible to dig through entirely the 2,500 years of tradition that are sedimented in our reading practices for texts of this sort, we have a couple of things going for us in the approach to Parmenides that make that task at least thinkable, if not easy. One is that we are not just familiar with but saturated by "end of philosophy" methodological scenarios: from Nietzsche, to Heidegger, to Derrida, it is quite natural for us to contemplate at least the prospect of post-disciplinary thinking. Therefore, it may be possible to contemplate the sort of pre-disciplinary thinking that Parmenides was inclined toward. Second, we live locally in an age that, via its preoccupations with poetics, has dramatically extended the range of our definition of poetry. And it is therefore quite easy to be reading someone like Parmenides primarily as a "sage" poet.

My first exposure to Parmenides was, though, in a history of philosophy textbook during my freshman year in college. That mechanism for telling a disciplinary history represents one very familiar cultural vehicle for transmitting a tradition: a series of authors are laid out sketchily, summarily, in sequence, most often in the framework of a dialectical narrative that is insistently progressive—all of which are stereotypically Western narrative structures. In such a narrative, for example, Parmenides has a very important and secure place to occupy and role to play. This, for example, is an excerpt from such a narrative that is much like the one I remember reading in my philosophy course:

> Heraclitus maintained that everything changes, and since philosophers love to argue, it is perhaps unsurprising that someone stated the exact opposite, namely, that nothing ever changes. This view was put forward by Parmenides, son of Pyres who came from Elea, a Greek foundation in southern Italy.
>
> . . .
>
> Parmenides stated that the senses deceive us and, hence, our perception of the world does not reflect the world as it really is. Instead, the real world is something above our apprehension and can only be apprehended through logic. His chief doctrine is that the only true being is "the One" which is indivisible and infinite in time and space. (Knierem, "Parmenides and Zeno")

Here we have an apparently clear distillation of Parmenides' intellectual project, viewed in panoramic mode from our vantage point 2,600 years in his foreground, his significance rendered by his advance from Heraclitus and, if we were to read further in this narrative, along a plot line certainly invisible to Parmenides at the time, his establishment of a position that Empedocles could parry, adding a new layer of complication and distinction. What more needs to be said, at least now, hundreds of significant moves later in the process? Parmenides agrees with Heraclitus that all is one but disagrees that change is the defining quality of being. We could read this summary a thousand times and read a thousand others like it and "know" something of consequence about Parmenides' place in the tradition. But do we really know anything about Parmenides, this author, this thinker, this poet, who was so oft-quoted by his contemporaries—which is, ironically, the only reason his work has survived, and only as a set of disconnected fragments that scholars try to piece together into a coherent sequence now, almost three millennia later? Not surprisingly, I could find no particular use for my "knowledge" of the Parmenides I came across in my philosophy class. What is left to say about, or say back to, a position as authoritative and static as this? Nothing.

What else might we do to engage with this thinker? Well, we could read his actual texts, which I did not get to do in my philosophy class but did end up doing for the first time about twenty years later, for specific reasons that I cannot recall, except that I took an interest in the pre-Socratics because of my interest in Greek rhetoric. So I read Parmenides' actual text, focusing most especially on those portions of it where he details his theory of changelessness, since this is what I was preconditioned to assume was his contribution to the field, and, therefore to the intellectual tradition. I remember reading and being taken by the following aphoristic assertion:

> Speaking and thinking are the same as WHAT IS.
> WHAT IS exists
> Nothing does not
> *Keep this before you.* (14, vi)

I suspect that somewhere in my head I interpreted and summarized these words for myself much like the earlier-cited source does, as follows:

> He argues that the perception of movement and change is an illusion and says that everything that is, has always been and will ever be, since it can always be thought and spoken of. The essence of this argument is: If you speak or think of something, the word or thought relates to something that actually exists, that is, both thought and language require objects outside themselves, other-

wise they would be inconceivable. Parmenides assumes a constant meaning of words and concludes from there that everything always exists and that there is no change, for everything can be thought of at all times.

Here we have Parmenides not by contrast with Heraclitus before him or Empedocles after, but, to some small degree at least, on his own terms. Now, I probably thought, I am in dialogue with Parmenides the thinker and not simply with his functionary role in the tradition's simplistic developmental narrative, written out as if the early Greeks were like "basic" writers of thought. I even mistakenly (as I realized later and as I'll clarify below) heard these words as being delivered authoritatively and directly through the voice of Parmenides himself, whom I had cast in my mind as an elder sage, handing down his hard-won wisdom directly to me, his prospective, and now more-willing-to-work student.

Just by coincidence, when my next contact with Parmenides came, a few years later, at a dark time for me, it was the second part of the aphorism I quote above, including the final imperative statement that stuck in my mind:

> WHAT IS exists
> Nothing does not
> *Keep this before you.* (14, vi)

What he had to say was, in fact, something at this particular moment in my life I wanted to find reason to believe, and Parmenides became a sort of screen for beginning to work out the process. So I went back to follow up on it. Right after this passage, the Parmenides I had constructed for my readerly self gets pretty agitated about the subject of nothingness;

> I bar you first from this road:
>   Do not think of Nothingness.
> And I bar you from the road the witless wander,
> the splaybrained masses without self-direction,
> deaf blind and astounded, the paranoid millions
> who compulsively confuse what is with what isn't,
> all of them moving on a retrograde road. (14, vi)

Yikes. This is pretty extreme and quite compelling. Parmenides, the teacher, speaking not directly to his reader but, I realized now, to the "young man," his student, in whose stead I could profitably stand as an auditor. I began to wonder how all of this might apply specifically to me. Clearly, I thought, we live in an extended era that is captivated in many ways by the allure of nothingness. The most stereotypical and accessible modern application of that term to the problem of "being," which is Parmenides' interest here, is, to me, in Sartre's *Being and Nothingness*, in which Sartre formulates human consciousness, the being-for-itself, as, by definition, absence and negation. Nothingness is its defining characteristic. Like many college students in the 1960s, I devoured existentialist philosophy, Sartre and Camus and Heidegger in particular, but also Nietzsche and de Beauvoir. I was raised on nothingness and had become thoroughly inured to it as an element of the human condition. But the concept wasn't serving me very well, and Parmenides was calling my attention to it.

Parmenides repeats the above structure, and his warning, multiple times in the poem, as in this example:

> *I am your teacher. Remember my words.*
> There are two ways for the seeker to understand the world.
> The first is
>   IT IS
> and that IT ISN'T cannot be.
> This route is committed to reality and truth
> The second is
>   IT ISN'T
> and that IT ISN'T must be
> No information comes back from this road. (12–13, ii)

As soon as I began to read the poem this way, as if Parmenides had something of consequence to say quite immediately to me, and as if I might gain something of consequence by trying to figure it out and say something back—not entirely either on his terms or on mine but on our terms, through this relationship—all of the above summaries of his thinking, including the last one, which prior to this seemed quite accurate and authoritative, became almost comically trivial. Even Heidegger, whom I greatly admire, and who strives over a lifetime to "recover" the originary genius of the pre-Socratics, especially in relation to the meaning of being, seems always to be grappling with and struggling against the affliction of nothingness that is built into his early ontological work. In his later years, in the series of brilliant and quite readable books on poetry and early Greek thinking, his method of recovery, a sort of hermeneutically grounded poetics, works better, but it has still its limitations in that it inhibits a chronotopically interactive relationship with the authors he seeks to understand.

In my next reading of Parmenides' poem, maybe ten years ago, I read it in a newer translation, by Stanley Lombardo, from which I am quoting all of my passages here, and I became simply entranced by the "proem" that introduces the substance of his message, a sort of strange, dream-inducing, dithyrambic, declamation that opens this way:

> The horses that take me to the ends of my mind
> were taking me now: the drivers had put me
> on the road to the Goddess, the manifest Way
> that leads the enlightened through every delusion. (11, i)

What riveted my attention to this part of the text was the striking metaphor of "the ends of my mind" that Lombardo uses in the first line. Most translations of Parmenides use the much less flashy and ambitious "as far as my heart desires," or some equivalent of that, in this spot. The effect of this new rendition was to jar me, as a reader, much more fully right now, into the position of the "I" who is the Goddess's student—not the kind of student who memorizes a textbook summary to take a test but the kind that signs on with a mentor to take a risk. The journey goes on, depicted in the most vivid and dramatic imagery of the "chariot" pulled by "wizard mares" and driven by "maidens," with red-hot axles "whin[ing] in the hubs," through "gates made of space-stuff," until "the Goddess / friendly / my right hand in hers" says to him, repeating the opening structure (11–12, i):

> The horses that take you to the ends of your mind
> have taken you here . . .
>   You are here to be taught,
> both the still heart of the Truth, unconcealed and committed,
> and human Opinion, on which there can be no reliance.
>   But you shall also learn this:
> how the Interpreted World really does exist,
> all of it one throughout space and time. (12, i)

This is one of the longest surviving sections of the poem, yet it is given, really, no place in any of the stereotypical disciplinary traditions indexed above. And it seems, further, to have no direct relationship to the "philosophical" significance of the argument. So why is this prologue here? Because when a reader turns himself over to the imperative of those lines, the poem can embody rather than explain the injunction Parmenides wants to deliver, a part of which says this:

> . . . Here again is the critical
> IT IS or IT ISN'T, and our decision has been
> to leave the latter unnamed, an unknowable nothing,
> not a true route at all,
> and to affirm the former as the authentic Way. (15, viii)

This is not Parmenides speaking indirectly to me as *his* student, which is the relationship I had always previously assumed, but the Goddess speaking directly to a version of Parmenides as the young man who needs her instruction, just as I do, and in whose stead I need to stand in order to get her message. The fact that I did not see this in my earlier readings of the poem was in part my own fault. It's abundantly clear in the text. But my misreading is in part, I want to argue, a consequence of the distorting effects of the tradition through which the transaction was commodified: Here we have Parmenides; he owns the Original Brand Monism Stand, down on West Philosophy Boulevard, right between Heraclitus, purveyor of pluralism, and Empedocles, the great mediator. It's a pretty long stretch from there to the young man in a mantric trance led off in cosmic chariot to be let in on the most basic secret of the meaning of life by a beautiful goddess, a stretch it is not surprising it might take a reader some time, and a few re-readings, to navigate.

The transaction with Parmenides is not a simple tutorial relationship with an elder sage delivering, secondhand, the wisdom he acquired by journeying as far as his heart desired. It is a peer relationship with Parmenides' alter-ego, who is hearing the "truth" for the first time, directly from the Goddess who sponsored his journey to the ends of his mind. Parmenides crafts this sort of engagement into the text by allowing the Goddess to address her wisdom directly the "young man" whom she "welcome[s]" and invites to "be glad" (12, i). In other words, he gives us a position to stand in to hear not his but *her* words with force. The Goddess is the "teacher;" Parmenides is, as our agent, "here to be taught," and we join the proceedings actively, assuming we are willing as well to follow to the ends of our minds (12, i). Meaning, and its inherent authority, is not regulated in this case by linguistics but by rhetoric. We, as readers, are invited to play the role of the "seeker," to enter into the play of authority in the argument, not just as equivalents of Parmenides' student, noble as that position might be, but as stand-ins for Parmenides himself, who offers us this space to inhabit and, further, gives us a way to embody ourselves quite fully there. And it is only by reading and re-reading him as a poet that I found it possible to get to this point.

Many of the poems I've been writing about are similarly complex in their rhetorical dynamics. Wordsworth's "Tintern Abbey" is deflected toward us through his sister, Dorothy, who is its primary intended auditor, her role there so strong I cannot help but read his "Ode" through a comparably refracting extrinsic lens. We miss a lot of the poem's poignancy if we don't hear Wordsworth talking to us, and himself, through her. Coleridge has the mariner tell his tale to the wedding guest, who is our, and perhaps his, proxy, via whom we all (including, I think, Coleridge himself, in an odd doubling back on his own authorial status) stand to learn the mariner's lesson. If we are to believe the various descriptions of Coleridge later in his life, it seems he should have listened more closely to what he had to say to himself through his alter-ego here. Whitman's "I" in "Song of Myself" is, finally, the exact opposite of the egoistic I of the lyric tradition, but is, rather, ecstatic in precisely its root sense: the I becomes, paradoxically, the vehicle for standing outside of the I, an amazing duplicity. And in the poem immediately in question, Parmenides is the student who is being taught teaching us. In all of these cases, the univocal authors so crucial to the teleology of the textbook timeline begin to replicate and complicate in the most interesting ways: as soon as we read them poetically rather than summarily. In that respect, they are much more like real people, and like us, than like the stripped down, polished versions that get handed down to us via the tradition, which tends to simplify, isolate, and magnify them, until, over time, they become almost superhuman—not just qualitatively but quintessentially different from us.

When I started my first college philosophy course, I was quite naïve. I fully expected to be reading texts that would thrill me with varying accounts of our culture's available wisdom about the "authentic Way" of Parmenides' poem. What I wanted were secrets to the meaning of life. I was sorely disappointed. We read summaries and snippets of the "great" works, but they came across not so much as simply packaged, which they were, but as vacuous, devoid of any energy or ultimate significance, just like the empty shells of cicadas littering the street. That was how I first came to hear about Parmenides, as a kind of cartoonish link between Heraclitus and Empedocles, who were equally cartoonish in this presentation. This, I thought, is the best we have to offer? I could think this stuff up in a couple of hours. It took me almost thirty years to finally get back to Parmenides, not just return to him, to engage him, to be thrilled by him. That is what is often missing in the way we teach and learn about the great poets. And by its absence, they are made no longer great.

Every time we stand before a text, approaching it as a reader, we negotiate—almost entirely in tacit and invisible ways—a relationship not just with the past but with the future. This relationship depends for its efficacy on a whole set of assumptions—again, almost entirely tacit and invisible—about temporal sequence, what it is and how it moves. This set of assumptions subtends even our notion of what is "past" in relation to where we are and where we are going, at least with this text, which remains at our approach entirely in our future, approaching *us*, reaching out to be met. This is our "position" when we sit down to read a poet. Whether we end up grasping anything from our side of that transaction depends, as I tell my freshmen, on whether and how we choose to make use of, for our own purposes, the words we read.

Four ❧ Preaching to the Birds

I DID NOT EXPECT TO TURN TO John Stuart Mill, of all people, as a help-mate in concluding my thinking about the value of poetry. I first en-countered his work in the college English class I wrote about earlier: Both Mill's "Autobiography" (a short excerpt) and "What Is Poetry?" (the first half of his "Thoughts on Poetry and its Varieties") were included in the *Norton Anthology of English Literature*. I don't keep many books, but for some reason I still have that one. I remember that I felt a mild sort of interest in Mill. But I specifically did not like his conception of the role of poetry in the economy of life. The image that stuck in my mind—I'm not sure if I concocted it from reading Mill or borrowed it from a commentator on Mill—was of a bedraggled businessman coming home tired and mildly depressed at the end of a productive day of money-making and retreating to his attic to read some poems as a solace for his soul, a kind of pleasing distraction to erase the harsher memory of the day just played out and to prepare a firm enough frame to support him through the one to come. Po-etry as a dry martini. It reminded me of the companion nineteenth-century cliché of the light-deprived, garret-ridden poet parsing out poems in ut-ter isolation. When I first read Mill, I was deep into the dramatic, high-pressure politics of the day. I was not writing political poetry. But I read and admired the poets who did, like Amiri Baraka and Daniel Berrigan, for example. Mill's paradigm seemed utterly afflicted by, as it remained entirely unconscious of, the British class dynamic: the poor starving artist providing beautiful artifacts for the solace of world-weary wealth-mongers.

A few years ago, I was preparing materials for an Introduction to Criti-cal Reading class I was teaching. We were discussing Whitman's *Leaves of Grass,* the preface of which is almost as explosive as the poems that follow it. In that preface, Whitman proffers a sweeping and exuberant statement on behalf of the poet of democracy, investing the poet with extraordinary pow-ers as a political, social, and cultural force to be reckoned with. I wanted to be sure that the class knew this was an apotheosized conception of the poet, that it took its place at the time among a pretty wide array of similarly gran-diose conceptions of the poet. So I put together a little handout of passages I took from other sources: Wordsworth's description of the poetic process from the preface to the third edition of *Lyrical Ballads,* Coleridge's defini-tion of imagination from *Biographia Literaria,* the soaring closing lines of Shelley's "A Defense of Poetry." I decided, out of the blue, to look again at Mill, to extract what I expected would be much more conservative defini-tion. I was surprised by what I found:

> [T]he word "poetry" imports something quite peculiar in its nature; something which may exist in what is called prose as well as in verse; something which does not even require the instrument of words, but can speak through the other audible symbols called musical sounds, and even through the visible ones which are the language of sculpture, painting, and architecture . . . (63)

> One may write genuine poetry, and not be a poet; for whosoever writes out truly any human feeling, writes poetry. (79)

These two passages struck me most because they offer a Janus-like face for framing out what is, for most poets, an almost inevitable practical problem concerning the manner in which the role of "poet" is assimilated as a func-tion of personal identity. One way of putting it might be this: Does one need to be writing, or at least trying to write, poems, actual poems, things that would be recognized in some potentially public way as poems, in order to be a poet? In the most obvious sense, the answer is no. No poet can write poems, or be working toward writing poems, all the time. It's just not possible. There are always interims, down times. But what if one who has been writing poems for some time, who thinks of himself as a "poet," perhaps is even recognized as such in some way, either can't or won't write poems for a year, or two years, or five years, or ten years? Arthur Rimbaud comes to mind as an extreme example in this case, a poet who just opted out. Is there a point at which, absent actual production, a poet ceases to *be* a poet?

Almost every poet at some point goes through a dry spell of this sort. It may be self-imposed or unbidden. But it happens. Wordsworth, in the two poems that most interest me in this project, is a very good example of a poet afflicted by, on one hand, a series of temporary creative absences and, on the other, by a much deeper and more troublesome loss of powers associated simply with aging. In "Tintern Abbey" we have a Wordsworth who has spent "five summers, with the length of five long winters . . . in lonely rooms, and 'mid the din / Of towns and cities" (301, lines 1–2, 26–27). During this ungenerative time his greatest achievement seems to have been feeling "unremembered pleasure" and "[h]is little nameless, unremembered, acts / of kindness and of love" (301, 31–34). The failure of memory here seems almost complete, and quite odd, as if all the things that most matter have somehow receded from consciousness to the nether world of an amnesiac. This is a theme he returns to again at the end of the poem when he is already forecasting his sister's similar decline, "When these wild ecstasies shall be matured / into a sober pleasure; when thy mind / Shall be a mansion for all lovely forms, / Thy memory be as a dwelling place / For all sweet sounds and harmonies" (302, 138–42). The metaphors of her mind as a mansion in which are stored all of the lovely, but now lifeless, forms, and of her memory as a dwelling where all the absent sounds and harmonies are archived, are, to me at least, quite disturbing. I imagine poor, dotty Dorothy tottering around a moldering museum-like mental attic looking in on her memories of things past, room by room, trying to resuscitate her lost youth. Such a "mansion" might become for her, as it already, it seems, has become for her brother, a buffer against "solitude, or fear or pain or grief" (303, 143). But it's not a cure for them. Here is a mode of poetry that has nothing to do with writing poems, at least for Wordsworth in that dim interim he must endure between his visits to this exhilarating site.

The same sort of thing happens in the "Ode." Here, for example, in the penultimate stanza, the birds are his audience and the message is the same:

Then sing, ye Birds, sing, sing a joyous song!
  And let the young Lambs bound
  As to the tabor's sound!
We in thought will join your throng

. . . .

  Though nothing can bring back the hour
Of splendour in the grass, of glory in the flower;
  We will grieve not, rather find
  Strength in what remains behind

. . . .

  In the faith that looks through death,
In years that bring the philosophic mind. (333, 168–86)

This poem is clearly not (ironically) the product of a dryly "philosophic mind," as are, to my ear at least, certain sections of *The Prelude*, being composed and revised contemporaneously (though it wasn't published until after his death, in 1850). It is lush and sensuous and beautiful. Wordsworth seems to have a gift for writing a great poem about the impossibility of writing as great a poem as he could have if only he still had "the glory and the dream." Thomas Carlyle's portrait of Wordsworth when he was in his seventies is of a poet with great pride, arrogance, even. No poet Carlyle could mention, not even Shakespeare, was worthy of Wordsworth's full approbation. Carlyle concluded, with a diminished sense of Wordsworth as a person, that "of transcendent unlimited there was, to [Wordsworth] probably but one specimen known, Wordsworth himself!" (*R*, 334). What better way to keep reinforcing such self-aggrandizement than to write a fabulous poem while claiming that one's powers so were dramatically diminished by time that it is a mere shadow of what it could have been, if only . . . ? On the other hand, there is Mill's assessment, that Wordsworth was not really a naturally gifted, "born," poet but one who achieved his effects with earned expertise and hard work. This is the opposite side of the self-effacements that erupt all over his poems, and it creates the opposite effect: an obvious companionability with his reader, who senses on some level, as Mill seems to have, that he, too, could create something like this if he just worked at it long and hard enough. As Mill says, "There is an air of calm deliberateness about all he writes, which is not characteristic of the poetic temperament. His poetry seems one thing, himself, another. He seems to be poetical because he wills to be so, not because he cannot help it" (84). Either way—whether Wordsworth is pulling our legs about his lost gifts or just working his ass off to get the poem right—I take his point: There is a big difference between the heart that "leaps up" when it beholds "a rainbow in the sky" and one that "can give / Thoughts that do often lie too deep for tears."

These are the private, inner struggles of a poet trying to grapple with his own identity *as* a poet. There is also an interesting public aspect to his problem, one that is most visible to me in the prefaces to the first two editions of *Lyrical Ballads*. In the first edition (1798), for example, Wordsworth and Coleridge don't even put their names on the frontispiece. And Wordsworth's brief preface is almost comically defensive, even about the degree to which the contents of the book might be perceived as poems: "Readers accustomed to the gaudiness and inane phraseology of many modern writers, if they persist in reading this book to its conclusion, will perhaps frequently have to struggle with feelings of strangeness and aukwardness: they will look round for poetry and will be induced to enquire by what species of courtesy these attempts can be permitted to assume that title. It is desirable that such readers, for their own sakes, should not suffer the solitary word Poetry, a word of very disputed meaning, to stand in the way of their gratification" (*LB* i–ii).

These are young men who, though they want very much to *be* poets, are deeply concerned about the prospects for their being *seen* as such. This takes us to the other side of Mill's equation for calibrating the poet, the opposite profile of the Janus-like face: "One may write genuine poetry and not be a poet"—or at least not be perceived as such by those temporarily authorized to make such determinations, whoever they might happen to be (and it varies a lot) at any given place and time. And I'm tempted to think (though he remains cryptic in this regard) that Mill might also be indicating that is possible to be recognized as a poet by these same powers that be and not be capable of writing genuine poems. I see Wordsworth and Coleridge, like most unrecognized young poets, as being afflicted by compounded crises of identity as they set their first book a-sail. And it is not much of a stretch for me to imagine (as it might not also have been for them) this first book failing, being completely ignored, simply disappearing into oblivion. How the authors would have responded to that is impossible to know. That's not what happened. Maybe they would have slinked off into anonymous silence. More likely they would have regrouped and tried again, in tandem or separately. But the timing of their initial enterprise seems to have been exactly right and the book hit it big. Or at least "big" by first-book standards: They got a few mixed to good reviews. In any case, just a couple of years later, in the 1800 edition, you have the emboldened authors announcing themselves by name. You have Wordsworth expounding at great length and with great confidence about all manner of things pertinent to what poetry is, where it comes from, and who this figure of the poet is who can produce such things. It's an amazing turnaround, driven, at least to some extent, I have to think, by the public reception (mild and mixed as it might have been) of their first edition. By 1802, a mere four years after the initial, timid declarations of the first edition, Wordsworth's now extensively supplemented preface is fully formed and permanently ensconced in the canon of English poetics.

Whitman offers another take on this problem of establishing a poetic identity. In the first edition of *Leaves of Grass* he takes the opposite tack from Wordsworth. Though he doesn't name himself on the frontispiece, he does later in the poem. And in his long and exuberant preface, he certainly declares himself as a poetic force, defining the figure of the poet he purports to promote and incarnate in the most intense and ambitious forms. There is not a whit of defensiveness in this presentation, unless you count being grandiose as, perhaps, the ultimate form of self-defense. The problem here is a little different: How did Walter Whitman, a marginally successful newspaper man, turn himself into Walt Whitman, the most amazing poet of his day. Was he always a poet in waiting, or did he suddenly become one? Again, it's possible for me to imagine a scenario in which Whitman's first book would have been either entirely ignored, as not-poetry in the first place, or as so scandalous in its content that it would be abhorred and forced into (historical) silence. But something else happened that is as difficult to fully account for as the original problem of how he wrote the thing in the first place: He received a brief but enthusiastic letter of endorsement from Emerson, which he made famous by appending it to his next edition of *Leaves of Grass*. But, curiously, Emerson never really calls his work poetry. It is "wit and wisdom" (*LG*, back cover), which is something different. This apparent slight did not seem to diminish Whitman's confidence or deter his progress. He had, I'm sure, already read Emerson's very traditional and much less expansive poems and may have been grateful not to have his own lumped in the same category, though his own typically voluminous reply to Emerson's brief and elegant missive, with its repeated deferences to his "master," shows not even a hint of a skepticism of this sort.

♣

THE GENERAL THEME OF THIS CHAPTER has in part to do with the exotic appeal of the poet and in part with the problem of finding an audience

willing to take seriously what he has to say. I offer one of my own poems,
"Morning Song 3," to open a way for thinking about these things:

> This morning
> all the bluebirds I ever knew
> (and that's a lot of them)
> stopped by my place just
> to sit around and sing.
>
> I couldn't figure it.
> I was no place they should be.
> But they were there. Not just
> like I was remembering.
> Like for real.
>
> Pretty soon it was "blue"
> this and "blue" that and
> "blue" them and "blue" me
> until there were more
> blues in that room than
> all the music I knew.
> Or than the sky.
>
> I rocked back and forth
> in my chair thinking:
> they say the Eastern Bluebird
> is nearly extinct, and most of
> this month I believed it.
> Now I have to wonder.
>
> On my way to work
> their cheerful, delicate voices
> diminished as I walked
> till all I heard was traffic
> or the wind, which seemed
> to want to wonder
> how any day could start
> so blue and come so soon
> to this.

This morning I had to take my daughter to the art building on the University of Pittsburgh campus for a Saturday class. While I waited for her, I walked around the permanent gallery on the first floor, which contains a number of exact replicas of large-scale Italian frescos and paintings from the fourteenth and fifteenth century. One of them struck me especially, and seems now pertinent to this conversation. It was a large (maybe eight feet by twelve feet) fresco titled *St. Francis of Assisi Preaching to the Birds*, an early fourteenth-century painting from the church that houses the remains of St. Francis. The style is simple and rustic, typical of the period. In the lower left-hand quadrant is St. Francis, leaning forward a bit, and "preaching" to an assortment of birds lined up on the ground with a few more flying in, a bit late for "class." Behind him is a colleague monk of his, dressed in the same brown hooded robe, kind of a large guy, with an expression on his face that says either: "Wow, this is amazing!" or "God, what the hell is wrong with this guy?"

If the only reason for reading great poems were to come to "understand" what they "mean" in a certifiably academic manner, they would still have some considerable value, as cultural capital, for example, or as a facilitator for social prestige. A dean (whose disciplinary background was in the social sciences) at one of the universities where I used to work actually argued that the value of English courses was in fact that they provided one with intelligent-sounding material to use at cocktail parties. But the reason I keep reading poems with vigor, and would do so even if I had absolutely no need to write about them for professional purposes, goes beyond that. So I come back over and over, like one of St. Francis's birds, to listen to each of my favorite poets preach.

One term we have for characterizing a preacher of this sort is "sage." The figure of the sage is generally alien to the American poetic tradition. One striking exception, to my way of reading, is Stephen Crane, who wrote all of those short, gnomic poems at the end of the nineteenth century. Some of them he even peoples with a character he calls the sage (or the "seer" or the "learned one"), as in the following:

> The sage lectured brilliantly.
> Before him, two images:
> "Now this one is the devil,
> And this one is me."
> He turned away.

> Then a cunning pupil
> Changed the positions.
> Turned the sage again:
> "Now this one is the devil,
> And this one is me."
> The pupils sat, all grinning,
> And rejoiced in the game.
> But the sage was a sage. (64)

This is classic Crane: the ins and outs, the ambivalences, and especially, distinctively, the darkly comic twist at the end. I've always been especially attracted to poets like Crane who are both scary and funny at the same time, who have a kind of over-the-top darkness to their vision. There's a very fine line here. Don't go far enough and the poem is threatened by simple, sappy sentimentality; go too far and it's threatened by equally simple, sappy cynicism; either of which is too trivial, by definition, to embody the sort of wisdom that defines the currency of the sage. To me, sentimentality and cynicism are the two great polar threats to both the poet and his "life." But when I'm writing poems, unless I'm teetering dangerously at one of these edges—or, ideally, at different points of the poem, both edges—risking everything with one slip, I am less engaged, less intrigued, less compelled by the process. I want to push a thought just to the edge of failure and, at the last second, keep it back. The poets who, from my point of view, do this best were working in America in the latter half of the nineteenth century: Emily Dickinson and, especially, Crane who is the epitome, to me, of getting it just right in this specific way. Take, for example, his most famous poem, about the ball of gold:

> A man saw a ball of gold in the sky;
> He climbed for it,
> And eventually he achieved it—
> It was clay.
>
> Now this is the strange part:
> When the man went to the earth
> And looked again,
> Lo, there was the ball of gold.
> Now this is the strange part:
> It was a ball of gold.
> Aye, by the heavens, it was a ball of gold. (36)

As is the case in many of his best poems, there are three stages to be traversed on the way to his wisdom. Here, for example, the first four lines are simply a nice rendition of a common cliché: What we strive for turns out, quite often, to be empty and illusory in its nature. And we don't find this out until we get there. Crane does it succinctly, but everyone already knows the commonplace. So at that point it's not much of a poem. Then there is the first "strange part": When the man abandons his ball of gold and goes back to the longer perspective, it appears to be exactly what he originally thought it was. At this point, he is vexed in a very specific way, and he has two quite familiar choices, a sentimental one and a cynical one: He will conclude either that he was right the first time about the ball's value and mistaken in his up-close assessment of it (and now, having acquired and then abandoned it he must start over again, feeling like a fool); or (more likely) that he was wrong the first time and can simply walk away gloating, to some extent, that he will not be fooled again (though also feeling at least a little irritated about having wasted time chasing it—instead of, for example, taking to heart the cultural cliché about the suspect quality of distant balls of gold). This is a somewhat more interesting thought and poem. Then, though, as is typical for Crane at his best, there is the *second* "strange part." It *was*, in fact, a genuine ball of gold. Even the heavens say so. The stakes are raised considerably. The man can no longer make an arbitrary choice based on his underlying temperament. He has to make a moral choice, depending not on the basis of his own judgment but on whether or not he trusts "the heavens." He can believe the heavens, and start over, hoping, praying maybe, that he can acquire the precious object again, which he will then most assuredly recognize as a ball of gold. In other words, his faith in his own senses, in himself really, will have been seriously compromised and can never be fully recovered, no matter how it turns out on the other end: Even if the ball is clay, he will have to believe it is gold. Or he can walk away based on his own initial judgment but, as a consequence, will have to seriously question, if not abandon entirely, his faith in the wisdom of "the heavens," which can never be fully recovered no matter how things work out on his end. Both of his options in this "second strange" part have a chilling, Sisyphean aspect to them; and either way there is, as Sartre might say, "no exit."

So to whom is Crane speaking in the final two lines of this poem, or the final line of the "sage" poem above? Clearly he is not simply addressing the "pupils" or the "man," all of whom remain captive to the inner workings of the worlds of their poems in ways that would make it quite difficult to "learn" from them. And he is not simply addressing us, as readers, either, at least not in terms that imply our freedom from the ironies that afflict the decisions available to the poems' primary foils. He carves out an anomalous space for us to inhabit, a space from which we can learn something, if we will allow ourselves to get to "the second strange part" of the situations in which we find ourselves, eschewing the kind of sentimentality that promotes victimhood or the kind of cynicism that promotes victimization. But, in the end, we get no real solutions to the riddles at hand.

The "Ancient Mariner" operates with a similar dynamic. Coleridge offers us the space of the grudgingly resistant wedding guest, in whose stead we can stand to receive whatever it is that is sage in the final advice of the mariner. Apparently, in the framework of the poem, it hits with enough impact to make the guest a "sadder and a wiser man." Should we choose to stand in his place we can, maybe, get there, too, "the morrow morn." In "Tintern Abbey," Wordsworth similarly provides us with his absent sister as a place to stand. As the poem closes, her emblematic function becomes abundantly clear:

> For thou art with me, here, upon the banks
> Of this fair river; thou, my dearest Friend,
> My dear, dear Friend; and in thy voice I catch
> The language of my former heart, and read
> My former pleasures in the shooting lights
> Of thy wild eyes. . . (302–3, 114–19)

When we overhear Dorothy overhearing the poem being addressed to her, oddly enough, it seems to absorb us also in its sphere—upliftingly, I'd say, to the extent that it makes us feel both companionable with William, who includes us integrally in his recollection of the "green pastoral landscape" (303, 158), and comparable to Dorothy, who is still unsullied by his "sad perplexity" (302, 60).

Unlike Wordsworth, who withholds his direct address to Dorothy, and his indirect address to us, until the poem's end, Whitman, characteristically, includes us immediately and directly, in the "you" that appears in the second line and is repeated over and over throughout the poem. This "you" operates not so much to define us as a separate figure in the dialogical relationship, but to blur the identity-based lines of demarcation between author and reader, all in a most ennobling and pleasant way. Pretty soon (by the next line) "every atom that belongs to" Whitman, "belongs as well" to me. That's pretty impressive. One of the primary salutary effects of all of this is the correlative invitation not to master the "meaning" of his poem but to "possess the origin of all poems." Then,

> You shall no longer take things at second or third hand . . . . nor
>   look through the eyes of the dead . . . . nor feed on the specters
>   in books,
> You shall not look through my eyes either, nor take things from me,
> You shall listen to all sides and filter them from yourself. (29, 27–29)

Basically, by listening to his poem, you can come to write your own. Not his, not like his, yours.

I TAUGHT MY FIRST CREATIVE WRITING workshop in 1978. I had never taken such a workshop myself, but I had absorbed from the general writerly culture a clear sense of how the enterprise was supposed to operate. Roughly speaking, students brought in their work, read it to the group without any commentary of their own, and got immediate, spontaneous feedback, mostly critical, from their peers. The instructor-writer would then chime in with a final (sometimes summative, sometimes definitive) commentary. This sort of pedagogy, so different from the ones that dominate in the teaching of literature and composition, my primary areas, had a long and noble history in the creative arena, more craft-oriented, and guild-building in its ambitions. So that's how I set mine up, too. With two crucial exceptions. First, I wanted to minimize the "definitive" potential of my commentary and to foster a sense of authority and collegiality among the group. So instead of sitting at the table—actually four tables assembled into a large square, the group seated around them, everyone able to see everyone else—I sat off to the side in a separate chair and made no comments at all on the student-produced poems. I thought at the time this was a great innovation. The group, on the other hand found it quite unnerving, almost creepy, as if I were more voyeur than guide. In any case, I was smart enough to abandon that particular technique after a few tense weeks. Second, I decided to include a lot of reading, all books by contemporary authors, most quite famous, the sort of work I assumed everyone was already reading. We discussed these works at some depth in terms of approach, technique, etc., for about half of each class session. This, too, was not well received by the group, mostly juniors and seniors who were used to having their own poems at the center of the discussions. They complained about the distracting effect of this reading, mildly at first, then more pointedly. A few weeks into the course it all came to a head. One of the women in the group just erupted, quite fiercely: "I don't want to spend my time reading these poets," she said. "It contaminates my originality." The rest of the group nodded or commented approvingly. I was stunned. That was an argument, given my own experience as a reader, that would never have crossed my mind. I knew I had to say or do something right then. I figured if I just backed down I would both lose the group and abandon one of my most basic writerly principles: You need to read good poets to become one. And I knew if I just said we were going to keep doing it and they could like it or lump it, the effect would be much the same. Teaching is like everything else in life. Most of the time you think of the exact right thing to say or do an hour, a day, or a week too late. Luckily for me, this was not one of those times.

I told them all to take out the poems they had brought in for that day's workshop. I asked them who had written poems of less than twenty-five lines. All raised their hands. I asked them who had written lyric poems grounded in their own personal experiences or feelings. All raised their hands. I asked them who had written poems with irregular line lengths and without end-rhymes. All raised their hands. And I asked them who had written poems that were driven primarily by images. Again, all raised their hands. I then asked what I wanted them to be thinking about through our discussions of these books: Where were we all getting essentially the same poetic method from? Why were we all writing variations on the same "workshop" poem that dominated the late 1970s? Certainly they didn't all invent this mode ex nihilo? So where did it come from? That started a grudging discussion about reading poets, as we looked for ways to think about the potential *value* of "contamination" and the *limits* of "originality."

All poets work at a specific historical moment. There is an ideology of production that tends to dominate at that moment, just as there is a dominant ideology of reception. There is a marketplace inclined to reflect that ideology, sometimes quite stringently. And there are undercurrents of resistance that take their shapes quite precisely in response to that ideology. A writer can go with or against the grain. But grain there is. And we at that table are as captive to it as anyone else. No poet's originality is ever uncontaminated, most especially if you are in an advanced poetry workshop, which enforces a strict discipline of its own. One interesting thing we could have talked about in that class but didn't was how this young poet inherited the notion that she could be completely original. Some of it comes from the ways in which critical discourses and systems work to mystify the figure of the poet: for example, the way the New Criticism situated the poet—as a disembodied, oracular absence—at the very top of the status pyramid, with gradually expanding rows of interpreters descending below, first critics, then teachers, then, in masses at the bottom, students. But at least as much of this mystification comes from poets, through the ways they characterize themselves to the public, perpetuating the illusion of out-of-nowhere-ness in their creative processes.

One entry point into this side of the equation is the concept of poetic "genius" that was endemic in the nineteenth century, beginning with the very Romantic poets I so enjoyed as a teenager. The ambivalent relationship I have with my own identity as a poet can probably be traced, in part, to these poets, none of whom thought of himself and his vision as "small." Coleridge is probably the most notorious in this regard. He may not have invented the concept of poetic genius, but he certainly institutionalized it through his theoretical work. He uses the word itself countless times in his *Biographia*, sometimes routinely, sometimes to make technical distinctions. But he also helped to propagate the exoticism of the poet-genius through stories about his own creative episodes. Here, for example, is his explanation for how he came to write "Kubla Khan," the marvelous fragment he withheld from publication for almost twenty years:

> In the summer of the year 1797, the Author, then in ill health, had retired to a lonely farm-house between Porlock and Linton, on the Exmoor confines of Somerset and Devonshire. In consequence of a slight indisposition, an anodyne had been prescribed, from the effects of which he fell asleep in his chair at the moment that he was reading the following sentence, or words of the same substance, in *Purchas's Pilgrimage*: "Here the Khan Kubla commanded a palace to be built, and a stately garden thereunto. And thus ten miles of fertile ground were inclosed with a wall." The Author continued for about three hours in a profound sleep, at least of the external senses, during which time he has the most vivid confidence, that he could not have composed less than from two to three hundred lines; if that indeed can be called composition in which all the images rose up before him as *things*, with a parallel production of the correspondent expressions, without any sensation or consciousness of effort. On awakening he appeared to himself to have a distinct recollection of the whole, and taking his pen, ink, and paper, instantly and eagerly wrote down the lines that are here preserved. At

this moment he was unfortunately called out by a person on business from Porlock, and detained by him above an hour, and on his return to his room, found, to his no small surprise and mortification, that though he still retained some vague and dim recollection of the general purport of the vision, yet, with the exception of some eight or ten scattered lines and images, all the rest had passed away like the images on the surface of a stream into which a stone has been cast, but, alas! without the after restoration of the latter! (546)

Here we have "All the images arose up before him as things . . . without any sensation or consciousness of effort," the "person on business from Porlock" who breaks the spell, and the unfinished poem. Classic Coleridge. Genius. The final stanza of this poem presents an image of exactly the sort of poet who would write this way:

> A damsel with a dulcimer
> In a vision once I saw:
> It was an Abyssinian maid,
> And on her dulcimer she played,
> Singing of Mount Abora.
> Could I revive within me
> Her symphony and song,
> To such a deep delight 'twould win me,
> That with music loud and long,
> I would build that dome in air,
> That sunny dome! those caves of ice!
> And all who heard should see them there,
> And all should cry, Beware! Beware!
> His flashing eyes, his floating hair!
> Weave a circle round him thrice,
> And close your eyes with holy dread,
> For he on honey-dew hath fed,
> And drunk the milk of Paradise. (547)

A "damsel with a dulcimer," the "flashing eyes" and "floating hair," the "milk of Paradise"—that pretty much says it all, doesn't it, about the witchy gifts with which poets of genius are endowed?

On the American side, Edgar Allan Poe is similarly extravagant in his self-aggrandizements, but in exactly the opposite vein. While Coleridge is struggling out of a laudanum-induced dream to get down what few he can of the three hundred lines he originally envisioned, Poe is claiming to operate more like a finely tuned, well-oiled, poem-making machine than the groggy melancholic that is one of his popular images. "The Philosophy of Composition," which I mentioned in chapter 2, details what he claims to be his customary process:

> Most writers—poets in especial—prefer having it understood that they compose by a species of fine frenzy—an ecstatic intuition—
> . . .
>
> For my own part, I have neither sympathy with the repugnance alluded to, nor, at any time, the least difficulty in recalling to mind the progressive steps of any of my compositions; . . . [I]t will not be regarded as a breach of decorum on my part to show the *modus operandi* by which some one of my own works was put together. I select "The Raven" as most generally known. It is my design to render it manifest that no one point in its composition is referible either to accident or intuition—that the work proceeded, step by step, to its completion with the precision and rigid consequence of a mathematical problem. (2:260–61)

Poe then details the whole process, step by step, as one would present a mathematical demonstration: from "intention" through "impression" to "tone" to "idea." Only then, with all this analytic work done, does he actually put a word on the page: "nevermore," the refrain that drives the poem. There are a bunch of analytic steps after that, all before the bird comes in. The odd thing about this depiction of his method is that I find it both preposterous and completely plausible. Who could possibly compose a poem along the pristine lines of Aristotle's formulaic for producing a good play? Yet think how entranced and brilliant Poe must have been to make such pleasure-inducing streams of sound in his poems, like these incomparably sonorous lines from "Annabel Lee:"

> And neither the angels in heaven above,
>   Nor the demons down under the sea,
> Can ever dissever my soul from the soul
>   Of the beautiful Annabel Lee:
> . . . .
> And so, all the night-tide, I lie down by the side

> Of my darling—my darling—my life and my bride,
>   In the sepulcher there by the sea,
>   In her tomb by the sounding sea. (2:27–28)

So spooky and musical. What teenager with a latent sense of doom wouldn't be enamored by such grandiosity? I bring all of this up because my sense of what a poet is was deeply and unconsciously formed in this crucible of myths and moods. When I realized I could commune so easily and deeply with these larger-than-life creators, I felt enlarged myself. But when it came time later for me to write poems of my own, poems that turned out to be much smaller and more intimate in their features, range, and contours, I tended to question their genius.

I could go on and on about the aggrandized figure of the poet in Romantic lore: profligate, flamboyant George Gordon, Lord Byron with his incomparably wild, celebratory excesses; glamorous, firebrand Percy Bysshe Shelley gallivanting with his talented author-wife Mary; tragic, tubercular John Keats dying young; brash, oracular Walt Whitman claiming all manner of powers public and private for the citizen-poet. These are the poets with whom I spent my youth conversing. I didn't know all of the stories about them then, but I knew a few and could guess the rest. I wasn't intimidated or even that impressed. They just seemed invitingly over-the-top, quite unlike anyone I was going to meet on the streets of my hometown or like anyone I had any intention of growing up to be. My being "both in and out of the game" in that way is, to some extent, what has allowed me to so enjoy the time I spend in their company and to learn from them, to actually have new experiences of my own. In other words, it's their contamination that allows for my originality, which is what I was trying to get across to my class.

WHEN HE WAS TWENTY-ONE, John Stuart Mill fell into a deep depression, which has been fairly called a nervous breakdown. During this time, as I did under similar circumstances, he turned more and more to poetry to keep afloat and promote recovery. He outlines all of this in chapter 5 of his autobiography. The most important poet for him during this time was, not surprisingly, Wordsworth, who was himself afflicted by despairs that he wrote about, wrote through. And Wordsworth was, I suppose, especially appealing to Mill because he was not, in Mill's terms, a "natural" poet, but one who learned the art he practiced. Mill identified with that, even though he was not a poet himself. Or, maybe, borrowing some initiative from the Mill passage quoted previously, it is more accurate to say that Mill *might* be a poet who simply wasn't that great at writing poems.

I have had a varied and vexed relationship with my own creative work. I write quickly and easily when it comes, first drafts at least, which I then rework, sometimes assiduously. But there are long stretches where the poems simply don't come—or more accurately, they might come, but they don't work—and I've never been able to find any discipline or set of practices that can force it forward when it's not right there. It's a very fine line for me. The poems of mine that don't work look and sound very much like the ones that do. The difference to me is like the difference between the singing cicadas I talked about earlier and the empty shells they leave behind. The latter might look exactly like the former, but they are absent the one thing that most matters: life. One of the abiding conundrums for any writer is who should get to make that call. Who's to say, for example, if I'm right or wrong when I consign one poem to my revision queue and another to the trash? Why don't I consult other readers? Join a workshop? Get some outside judgment into my early process? I just don't and don't want to. Basically, I am very possessive of that specific authority and I don't brook well any advice along those lines. It's one of the reasons I avoided taking creative writing workshops while I was in school. I am already, I tell myself, in constant conversation with the best poets in history, and they give me constant advice, at least indirectly, about what makes a good poem. What could be better than that?

That's the major reason I have set up my professional life in such a way that it does not depend on the production of poems to be sustained. How could I, when the process is so unpredictable and unreliable? Because of all this, maintaining a clear distinction between the poet and the writing of publicly well-received poems has been crucial for me. And it has allowed me to be quite severe, when I wanted to be, in relation to the production and publication of individual poems. I sometimes go for very long stretches, years, without sending poems out for external review. And I have even forced myself to stop writing poetry completely on three separate occasions. Each time (excepting the last, so far) I started writing poems again after a few years, but in an entirely new way. I can and will account here for each of these cessations in autobiographical terms. It is harder for me to explain what regulates the larger rhythms of stopping and re-starting. There are just times when what I *always* seem to get from reading poets—more life—is not what I'm getting from writing my own poems. Instead of just enjoying the work, I make too much of it, get caught up in public or professional aspects of the process in ways that are out of all proportion, distorted, dead-ening. And I need to stop in order to right myself. In the economy that Mill lays out, it may be that for me to continue to survive *as* a poet, I need from time to time (sometimes for long stretches) to *not* write poems. Somehow, as Marcel Marceau says, "silence is full of music," and it produces a new music in its wake. I think Mill (and many other poets) would understand that paradox.

My first enforced silence of this sort occurred in early 1972, due to the reasons I described more briefly in chapter 2 and want to delve into in more detail here. I had the good fortune to have read an awful lot of truly great poetry very early on. I consumed it almost addictively for several years be-fore I wrote anything of my own that could be called a poem or started studying poetry in a seriously academic manner. When I began writing those poems of my own, I knew that my gifts were different—lighter, smaller-scaled—from the poets I had been reading. There is an expression in the Catholic calendar for what is called "ordinary time," the parts of the year not occupied by great figures and events. My poems, I have always felt, tend to exist in ordinary time, and they like it there. And I like them there. I might write some very good poems, I thought back then, which is what I have done, but they would not be of the scope or the magnitude of those I most enjoyed reading—more on the back end of the mariner's "things both great and small." I don't recall at all being humbled or even mildly depressed by that insight. The attitude that supports it is just built into my temperament, informing everything I do, so it just seemed obviously true to me.

In any case, around my sophomore year in college, feeling I had a very good grasp of poetry written in English from time immemorial to about 1940, I decided that I needed to find out what was going on among more contemporary poets. I threw myself into this endeavor feverishly, consum-ing everything I could get my hands on. Much of it was in the "confes-sional" mode that was dominant at the time. I read Robert Lowell, Sylvia Plath, Anne Sexton, a long, awesome, frighteningly beautiful dirge. Such music. Such misery. I also read a lot of surrealist poets, "concrete" poets, drug-inspired poets, Beat poets, projectivist poets, New York poets, femi-nist poets. I started to hang around with other young writers whose capacity for death, drugs, and alcohol was staggering to me. After a while I thought I was losing my mind. It was A. Alvarez's *The Savage God,* his (famous, back then) study of the relationship between poetry and suicide, that capped it all off for me. Shortly after the encounter in the bar that I detail in chapter 2, a very good friend of mine told me he wanted to be "the next Berryman," and he was willing to risk it all to get there. I found that statement very disquieting and it added a cautionary residue to my thinking about these matters.

I mention John Berryman here for a reason. In 1969, right around the time I was changing my major from physics to English, my brother decided to join the Book-of-the-Month Club, for which he would receive a number of free books—maybe six or seven—from a select list. He picked out the ones he wanted but was still a couple short. So he showed me the list and asked me to pick something. All I wanted right then was poetry, and the only poetry book on the list was John Berryman's *Dream Songs*. I had heard of Berryman, but hadn't read much of his work, and what I had read I didn't particularly like. But it was poetry. So I picked the book. When I read it for the first time, I was quite baffled—all the inverted syntax, the different voices, the quirky, compressed style. I read it once, fast, as was my style. I felt it was good, I was moved, but I didn't "understand" anything about it. So I read it again. Then again, over a period of a year or two. I came to love the book and Berryman's work generally. About five years later, I wrote my dissertation on *The Dream Songs*. In one of the most enjoyable and productive scholarly enterprises of my life, I wrote the whole thing over a summer, working from nine o'clock to five o'clock in a four-by-six, sunny window alcove in my apartment in Albany. Sometimes it is hard to predict where you'll end up when you start to read a poet.

After I graduated from college, I moved to Pittsburgh. I was unemployed for most of the next year, living in a dreary, dim apartment. I had been trying for months to establish a habit of writing, to see if I could really become a poet. By my sights, I produced just reams of daily drivel. This was a dark moment in American history and a dark time for me generally. I became discouraged about everything. On January 7, 1972, I was watching the *Evening News* with Walter Cronkite, rife as usual with grim images from Vietnam, and, to me, equally grim images of Richard Nixon. What could be worse than all that? Well, for me, what followed. The last item on the news that night, right before Cronkite's signature signoff, was his announcement of John Berryman's suicide. It was one sentence: "Today poet John Berryman jumped to his death from a bridge in Minneapolis to the frozen Mississippi. And that's the way it is . . ." I felt like someone had kicked me in the stomach. I went out for a long walk along the fringes of Frick Park, an urban park large and densely wooded enough to get lost in, as I had previously discovered. Then I came home and wrote the poem below, an elegy for John Berryman. Just wrote it out, pretty much as it is, all that futile daily writing grind having been, perhaps, nothing but preparation for this. And when it was done, I knew I was done writing poetry for a while.

A Way Down Note: for John Berryman

> It was wet & white & swift and where I am
> we don't know . . .
> —"Dream Song 28"

I

It is wet but hardly white
this bleak night. Snow
will not come. Clouds
moan their burdens
and snow will not come.

Frozen leaves skitter down
the street, armies of leaves
spreading the gray news
like gossip: "He dead, ain't he?
Mr. Bones and all of 'em: dead."

II

Dead. Dove
like a broken wing singing
to pieces. Today
picked his brains, his last song,
mercifully on the ice.

And the world remembered
in its way (somewhere between
Richard Nixon and nothing)
that Henry sang and
will not sing more.

Dead. A dreamer
gone to dreams.

III

Now putting on your tall hat
in the right place,

forgive us who live
without your suffering song.

Now, surely knowing
everything, be with us
when we cannot pray
your prayers.

    IV

A few bare trees file past:
old, gnarled, clattering tambourines,
black and mournful, clattering tambourines.
They do not speak.

But the leaves settle.
And snow falls
white and swift,
in mute praise.

The poem is full of allusions to Berryman's poems, which I felt was a kind of homage to him; and the "mute praise," I thought, would be my life, one I would live, not imperil, for poetry, which I knew I would always keep reading and decided I would try to teach. So I applied to graduate schools. I had been writing poetry reviews for *Best Sellers* for a couple of years—a wonderful learning experience for a young poet, this sitting down with something brand new and trying both to assess its significance and to locate it in a tradition, without any outside sources to consult for support—and I decided to focus on that kind of critical work for a while. I enjoyed it in part, at least, because I no longer had to think of myself as a potential competitor or wannabe for the great writers I got to introduce through my reviews. I felt a deep sense of freedom and relief. Within a couple of years, though, things had changed enough with me and with the world of contemporary poetry that I started up again, in a new mode, thankful that the culture of death was finally going out of fashion. The elegy to Berryman I had written was accepted by a small journal called *John Berryman Studies,* which went out of business the issue before my poem was scheduled to go into print. So it makes its debut here, almost forty years after I wrote it.

My second secession occurred some twenty years ago, in 1988. My daughter was two. I was about to turn forty. I had been trying to find outlets for my poetry, on and off, very haphazardly and, apparently, incompetently, since my early twenties. I had published about thirty poems, individually and in groups, but could not get any takers on my book-length submissions. I don't have any idea how many rejections I had received by then. Whatever it was, it was, at that moment, one too many. I was stressed, overworking, and well on my way to the "breakdown" I describe earlier. The "business" side of poetry, which I abhorred but felt I couldn't ignore, was turning my writing more and more into a chore. I knew I needed to opt out for a while. But I wanted to write one last poem as a swan song. I wrote it over a six-week period in a cozy upstairs study in the row house my wife and I bought just before our daughter, Bridget, was born. For me to get some uninterrupted time to write (primarily scholarship to build a portfolio in support of my impending case for tenure) we decided to hire some in-home childcare. Childcare was much less regulated and much harder to find back then. A friend was providing housing for a foreign student and suggested him to us. He was a young (early twenties) university student visiting from Poland looking to make a little money to support his studies here. He was thin, pale, and had longish, light-brown hair that hung down straight over his shoulders on both sides of his narrow face; he was very mild-mannered and spoke his limited English with a sharp Polish accent. I can't remember how to spell his name, but it was pronounced: Votzik Zribowsky. He was quite charming and we hired him to spend a few hours a day with Bridget while I wrote upstairs. His most memorable (for me) way of entertaining her was singing Polish drinking songs while they threw back shots of milk. Bridget loved it. I was working feverishly to finish an article at this time, right before Easter, I remember, a deadline having crept up too quickly. But my real preoccupation was the poem I was trying to write, one based on the myth of Daphne being turned into a tree by Zeus. The poem was keyed into a memory from my early youth concerning a specific, large tree that I had to walk past to get to a nearby creek. It was a perfect vehicle to carry this particular farewell to poetic composition. I would cease to be a poet, in all the public ways that were afflicting me, and become a silent poet, "like a tree, standing by the water." Here is the poem I wrote, called "For Daphne: On the Mornings After:"

I

She told me how in her day
it happened matter of factly:
some girl on her way, say,

to the well, stopped in her tracks,
legs stiff as stumps,
feet rooted to the ground;
and from fingertips clutching
into a cloudless, blue sky,
thousands of leaves puffed
from their buds at once.

The news spread fast:
proud parents announcing it,
a coming out of sorts;
brothers and sisters amazed
at the luck of such a great story
to tell to their friends at school;
her boyfriend, well, at a loss,
a little miffed, missing her.
Later, all the celebrating done,
everyone else home and asleep,
he'd hold her in his arms all night,
promise never to marry.

II

I couldn't have been more than
six or seven when I first heard you
murmuring from the old elm
I had to walk past on my way
to the creek to play.
For years I steered clear,
trying not to listen.
Then one morning, my mind
too much abuzz with wonder
to stay away, I clung to the trunk
hoping to seep like a dark stain
into the clean wood beneath.
That night your words
turned into flocks of birds
swarming wildly by moonlight
across savannas of empty sky.

III

Last week, on my way to work,
the hollow of my head filling up,
as usual, with a cloudless,
blue sky, two birds circling
without a place to settle,
my legs just suddenly stiffened;
tendrils descended from
my feet, holding me hard
to the earth; my arms,
flung up to steady myself,
locked upward, hands cupped
open like empty nests.

Clouds of doubts massed up,
passing in fast-forward,
rationales I ransacked
in my panic for an answer:
the inevitable and graceless
changes of age? the grappling
fingers of someone else's past?
death's staccato laughter?
Then the birds settled
and I heard again your words.

IV

I notice it now mostly mornings:
a little stiffness in my hips,
that ringing in my ears.
All day the birds busy themselves
with nesting. By night
they settle down to rest.

I hear only the ceaseless music
of their voices, or mine, singing
of loves lost and then recovered,
ever the same song, growing
simpler and more clear,
nearer to the light into which

we are always rising up or settling,
beyond which there is nothing more now
either one of us needs to say.

If ever there were a document that seeks to utter Bakhtin's impossible "ultimate word," this is it. The circular connection between youth and age, the fixity of the transformation, the blurring of gender distinctions, even species lines, as the poem proceeds, the singing voices that cannot be traced to a source, and, finally, simply the ceaseless music about which nothing more needs to be said. I like this poem for all of that, its transgressions, its ambitions, its contrarily tight form, clipped lines. Re-reading it now I almost can't believe it *wasn't* the last poem I ever wrote.

The poem is "rooted" in a strange experience I had as a child. To get to a spot my brothers and I liked to go to, you had to get over a high, wire fence. There was a hole in the fence at one point that was easy to get through, so that's where we always crossed. Just on the other side, there was a broad, tall tree, which I think of, in retrospect, as an elm, though it could have been anything. All I remember about it is its massive trunk. Whenever I got close to that tree I felt something like an electric charge or hum in my body, especially my head, a real physical sensation that seemed to be attracting me like a magnet, with an intense accompanying desire to be absorbed into the tree. At the time, I found this both exciting and scary, the prospect of being assumed into the tree. It reminds me a little of how Wordsworth must have felt on his way to school when he "grasped at a wall or a tree to recall [him]self from this abyss of idealism" (331). I understood clearly, even then, that this was quite odd, not normal, so I never told anyone about it, not even my brothers. For a while I thought I could make it stop by touching or holding the tree, which I tried a few times. It didn't work. So I decided to keep as much distance as I could between me and the tree as I went around it. After a couple of years the sensations went away. But I have carried with me always a great admiration for trees—their patience, their steadfastness, their tenacity, their quiet beauty, their silence—and a personal ambition to be similarly enduring, committed firmly to my spot from which, like this huge elm, I would "not be moved."

Apollo is, among other things, the god of poetry. The poem originated at a moment when, like Daphne, who had been inoculated by Cupid's arrow to instinctively resist Apollo's advances, I felt I had been chased around long enough. I was, like her, growing tired and slowing down, and I did not want to be "married" to this sort of "savage god" of song. Alvarez's suicidal scenario was not an issue this time. It was a growing frustration with the sort of inner death that occurs when you want something that you can't get for far too long; that comes from compulsion, obsession, which trap one in empty temporal spaces, spaces past that did not exist (and why not, one might legitimately wonder?) or spaces future that cannot and will not exist because the course of things necessary to support them has never emerged. The idea of turning into a tree looked as good to me as I'm sure it did to Daphne when she got tired of enduring Apollo's chase. I wrote this poem and didn't write another one for several years.

I quit writing poems again about ten years ago, in my early fifties. This time was different from the other two: instead of wanting simply to avert something negative, unhealthy, I wanted also to accomplish something positive, healthy, for myself. I had just started walking as one part of a multipronged regimen to cope with a combination of stress-related maladies. I had a variety of routes I walked daily up and down the hills of the Pittsburgh suburb where I live with my family. Every day I would see something that looked compelling to me for one reason or another—a tree in flower, a bird in flight, an angle of light. But I found myself repeatedly doing what I had always done, almost unconsciously, in situations of this sort. I'd look at the thing and a few words would start to emerge in my mind, the potential beginnings of a poem. They would rarely be interesting enough to me to pursue when I got home. But they kept distracting me from what I wanted to be doing, which was just to look at and see what I saw right there and then. Instead, within seconds, I was back inside my head messing with my words. I started thinking about how much of my adult life had been consumed in just this way: a second or two of attention out there in the world, and then hours inside my head with this inner stream of my own words, which started to feel to me just like the camera I described earlier, something standing in the way of what I wanted to connect more directly with, which was right in front of me.

I had a conversation pertinent to this with a colleague about twenty years ago. We were talking about William Blake's poems, and I made a comment about their cryptic brevity, which to me carried me toward the ineffable when I read them. My colleague reminded me that in postmodern critical systems there were no such things as ineffable meanings, that the primacy of language as a constitutive agent precluded the possibility of imagining the unsayable or of saying the unimaginable. My colleague said it all better than that, but that's the gist of it. I remember thinking, "Yes, that's right." And then, "Oh, man, no such thing as the ineffable? What a drag. I love the ineffable." It had always been one of my favorite places to be in my own inner world. And having it as an available category at least allowed me to continue to think that the fact I was unable to *say* everything I clearly thought I knew, to *write* everything I clearly knew I thought, was not necessarily to admit that my failures to make myself evident, and to find a receptive audience, were ultimate. Just because these things remained beyond my reach did not mean that they didn't exist in the first place. Importantly and more practically, I could continue to *be* a poet even though I wasn't being widely acknowledged *as* one. So the ineffable was crucial to my identity in this regard.

Here was another clear case in which a temporarily current critical ideology came into conflict with my preferred way of being. I think on some level I decided right then that I simply would not resign myself to a world where everything was effable. And when I started my long walks and saw those simple, amazing things, I wanted to try to recover the ineffable, at least at those moments. To do that, I knew, I would need to deter the first words' emergence, to keep my concentration and focus outside and in the present, and away from the inside urge to convert sensation into a figment of the past and future. It became a kind of mental discipline, a mode of meditation maybe, over and over, saying not-now, not-yet, to the words that floated up, on the assumption, or hope, that sooner or later another mode of writing poems would evolve, one that extended rather than disrupted my connection to the ineffable. I have over the years made small progress in this regard, but progress nonetheless. One of the costs has been in giving up the potential poems that might have evolved had I let their initial inklings take a foothold in my attention. The last poem I wrote before I started this process was not intentionally designed as a formal "ultimate word" as the previous poem was. But it captures the sense, or state, I wanted to get myself into in relation to immediate sensuous perception and the deeper realities of life:

WINTER SOLSTICE 1999

(with some fragments from Empedocles)

a roomful of pure moonlight
oozes over every
pore of my body
bathes me as if I were a child
peals of his laughter leak
like helium I hear

a little-boy voice squeak
parts of his heart healing . . .

he says to me:
shelter . . .
a silent
heart . . .
he says to me:
love . . .
tenacious
love . . .

he says to me:
there . . .
it is fixed
forever . . .

night after night I sit here
silent in the dark thinking
I am closer than ever now
to the last great nothing
these dreams keep leaving
my children build heavens
I try . . .

tonight I will hold myself
in my own warm arms
then let them come apart
riffle through pages scattered
around me on the floor
lift them up in big bunches
how slowly they float
back down, shining
with borrowed light

tonight I will write myself
a love poem
it will begin with the line
"a roomful of pure moonlight"
but it is not this poem

this poem is only
to help me
forget
what you thought
I was trying to say . . .

Just after I finished this poem I did a reading in a small gallery that was formerly a meat-packing house in the Lawrenceville section of Pittsburgh. I thought I'd test-drive the poem that night to see how it sounded. When I do a reading, I always script out, at least vaguely, some patter between poems, partly transitional, partly introductory, partly mood-lightening, both for the audience and for me. So before reading this poem, I said a few things about Empedocles (whose words appear in italics in the poem): how all that remains of his work, as is the case for the pre-Socratics generally, is an array of random fragments, which endure because they appear in other texts. Scholars then arrange these fragments in what they believe to be their most likely original sequence. In the translation I was reading at the time there were two consecutive pages (fragments 18 and 19) on which only these words remained: on the first, "love," and on the next, offset toward the middle of the page, "tenacious love." The effect of this accidental arrangement, I said, took my breath away every time I read it. And then I spontaneously happened onto a perfect punch line for my patter: "This is one of the most beautiful 'love poems' I have ever read. You take away 99 percent of Empedocles' words, and he's still a better poet than I am with all of my words still on the page." It got a genial, generous laugh from the group gathered that night, and from me, too. I knew that I had just read the last poem I was going to write for a while and was halfway through the last reading I was going to give for a while. I'm a pretty good reader of my own work, but I find the experience stressful. That night was different, so relaxed, so casual, so enjoyable. If my own "life of the author" were a movie, it would end that night, my walking out into the frigid January air, a few flakes of snow swirling. I haven't written a poem for years now. Not a full, "serious" poem, I mean, with scrupulous attention at the revision stage. Just little snippets I drop in a folder in my computer called "New Poems." There they sit, waiting. Yet I think of myself as, in some respects, more of a poet now than I did when I stopped writing poems. How can that be?

For one thing, my relationship with my work is more like that of a reader to an author, an other, a not-me. I recall, even re-read, my own poems to help me with my life. But it's more complicated than that, as in the above poem, where my position is neither author nor reader. For example, consider the two missing poems that haunt, and actually become more important than, the poem that houses them: Empedocles' poem, which has been mostly lost to time and is available only as a palimpsest implied by the fragments that remain; and the poem that "is not this poem," which can emerge only as the poem that is disclosed—by the process of its disclosure—helps the poet to forget what "you thought" he was "trying to say." The actual poem, the one I wrote and read, is induced from the outside-in, not just by the culturally inculcated, but hidden, desire to say what an audience expects to hear, or even by the literary conventions of the moment that regulate the marketplace, but also by the limitations of human discourse, which never seems capable of carrying the full weight we hope for it to bear. The actual poem, then, merely clears the way for the real poem, which requires no "trying" to say. This silent poem is not like the ones that Thomas Gray laments in "Elegy in a Country Churchyard," or that Virginia Woolf foregrounds through the figure of "Shakespeare's sister" in *A Room of One's Own*. Gray and Woolf mourn for those voices who, by the accidents of their social/historical circumstances, never had a chance to be heard, even by themselves. Neither is it like the ones that Emily Dickinson sewed together and squirreled away in a drawer. Those were ultimately found and heard, and even if they weren't, they were written, fully disclosed, by and to the poet who wrote them. And it is not like Empedocles' poem, which once was there and now is not. It is, though—this silent poem that is not there—the poem that makes me more of a poet than the one I actually wrote. Again: How can that be?

☙

AS I SAID, RIGHT AROUND THE TIME I wrote my last official poem, I started taking morning walks. Initially, I walked a mile or so by myself. Now it's about four miles, and I'm almost always accompanied by wife, Carol. We talk a lot on the walks, but there's a lot of very pleasant silence, too. I can honestly say that almost every day I see something, a little thing usually, that uplifts me in a very specific way, allowing me to experience something like what, a couple of millennia ago, Longinus called the sublime. In his essay, Longinus is most interested in detailing the sorts of rhetorical devices, especially figurative language, one can use to inspire sublimity in an audience. Tacit to this is the necessity to have had some sublime experience in the first place. If I wrote poems like Wordsworth did, long after the fact, the original emotion still intact enough to be "recollected in tranquility" as a first step in the process, I'd have no problem. But for me, it's either extend the experience for a while at the expense of the first emergent words, which are essential for its rendition into a poem, or stop the experience and start the poem right then. At least on these walks, my preference is for the former. I want to feel an intimate and immediate connection to something not-me. If it doesn't happen spontaneously, I'll initiate the "look" myself, like a Sartrean "gaze," I guess, but exactly the opposite in that its function and effect are toward connection, communion, rather than objectification, alienation. I try to resist as best I can the temptation to convert those moments into words, which are sometimes, for me, a greater threat, as a kind of self-inflicted temporal matrix, to "the visionary gleam" than the actual passage of time itself, which is inevitable and to a certain extent quite elegant in its own right, as the distinguishing feature of our experience of this particular world.

I've never been one to identify very closely with the "Child of joy" version of himself as a boy that Wordsworth seems to be lamenting the loss of in his "Ode." That's just not what my childhood was like. I did grow up in a rural environment, I spent a lot of my time with nature, as I still do. But my relationship with nature is much more casual and intimate, lighter, I think, than his. I am at ease in the presence of things, as I feel they are at ease in my presence, much more so than I am in most social situations. Many of my poems are animated by things natural—birds, trees, flowers, light, dark—sometimes as focal subjects, sometimes as background. None of these things come from a Nature that begins with a capital N, which seems to me to make both too much and too little of it. In any case, I just don't have in my own personal history any recollection of an idyllic time to which to hearken back. Maybe that's why, even though I'm nearing sixty as I write this, I don't feel afflicted by any deep longing for a lost "glory." It hasn't "passed away . . . from the earth," at least not in Wordsworth's terms, all this "happy Shepherd-boy" and "Darling of a pygmy size" stuff, which was never there in the first place (332). And, on the opposite end, I don't any longer find myself clutching toward the future, wishing that some sort of "celestial light" might someday shine down on me. Whatever great or small things might still happen will surprise me. Such illusive nostalgias— whether forward-looking or back—produce, I believe, either sentimentality or cynicism, along the same lines that I describe earlier, both of which I work to minimize. So this is a good time of life for me. On a daily basis I can have at least a brief real encounter with a life that seems quite like mine. It's right there coming toward me, waiting and wanting to be met. And part of making myself eligible to meet it—for now at least—involves keeping *my* words at bay. I'd much rather extend that moment or two of what I experience as radical freedom, complete play, than put a premature stop to it by converting it immediately into the currency of words. Do I experience such moments because I've read all these poets? Have I read all these poets because I experience such moments? Am I a poet because I experience such moments? Is writing poems about such moments something I've invested myself in and enjoyed? Is not writing poems about such moments an important part of my experience of them right now? These are all, to me, variations of the same question, the answer to which is yes.

I generally endorse the postmodernist notion that we swim in a sea of words that define us every which way. I understand we cannot totally opt out from that. But, for a moment or two, here and there, we are, I believe, both equipped for, and allowed to, come up for a breath of air. And at these moments we encounter the ineffable. I think of this state of mind as a very specific kind of innocence. I keep casting about among the poets I've read for an analogue, but I don't find a match. It is not at all, for example, like the mode of innocence that Blake depicts in his early songs under that nameplate. The figures there are both too pristine, like the "little lamb," and the contrary figures too darkly foreboding, like the chimney sweep. And it's not even like the more appealing Blakean concept of "organized innocence" that I remember first reading about, and being enamored of, in a footnote in my college *Norton*. Here the "contrary states" of naïve innocence and harsh experience are synthesized "by an act of imagination," to the "third state" (50). This kind of clumsy Hegelian dialectic seems to be more a concoction of subsequent scholars than of Blake. In any case, it's all too dry for what I have in mind. I like a little better the "radical innocence" that Yeats describes in "A Prayer for my Daughter," one in which hatred is "driven hence." As a consequence, the soul:

> . . . learns at last that it is self-delighting,
> Self-appeasing, self-affrighting,
> And that its own sweet will is Heaven's will (92, 67–69)

There's a lot to like about this way of defining innocence. But here Yeats proffers it only as a future hope for his infant daughter, in a scene eerily reminiscent of the one Coleridge sets for us in the sad and lovely "Frost at Midnight," where he hopes the "Great universal Teacher" will "mould" his son's "spirit, and by giving make it ask" (538). For Yeats, in his mid-fifties when he writes his poem for his daughter, his and Heaven's will are a quite a bit at odds. A "great gloom" (90, 8) afflicts his mind, which "has dried up of late" (91, 51). He's still ranting about his failed relationship with Maud Gonne, the love of his life. So let's just say his is not an innocence that ages well. Even the vehicles he recommends to enact it—"custom and . . . ceremony" (92, 77)—are afflicted by the strife of time and are largely dependent on language, which is time's primary province. All those not-nows and not-yets elbowing their way in to crowd out the now.

Still, I find myself thinking more and more about Yeats lately. He was my age and older when he wrote so many of his greatest poems, the opposite of that deeply ensconced cultural image of the "romantic" young poet fluorescing gloriously in his twenties and gradually flaring out, faltering, or, most mythically, dying young, before age has its way with his gifts. If Yeats had died at the age Keats did (twenty-six), or Shelley (thirty), or even Byron (thirty-six), he would be at best a secondary, if not forgotten, figure in the history of British literature, a nice book or two under his belt. To my way of reading, it's not until the *Green Helmet* volume, in 1910, when Yeats was forty-five, that he truly begins to hit his stride. And from there, the poems just get better and better, deeper, clearer, more complex, more beautiful, often more troubling, sometimes more serene, until he says, in "Sailing to Byzantium":

> An aged man is but a paltry thing,
> A tattered coat up on a stick, unless
> Soul clap its hands and sing, and louder sing . . . (102)

When I imagine myself coming back to writing poems, whenever that happens, I want to take full advantage of what age brings: the refined craftsmanship, which comes from years and years of assiduous attention to detail; but more importantly the wisdom, the clarity of vision, that great state of mind that Yeats describes in "Lapis Lazuli," of "gaiety transfiguring all that dread" (179). He ends that poem this way:

> On all the tragic scene they stare.
> . . . .
> Accomplished fingers begin to play.
> Their eyes mid many wrinkles, their eyes,
> Their ancient glittering eyes, are gay. (180)

Yeats in his later years may be looking at life and death, as he says, with a "cold eye." But, again, we have to think about "cold" in a whole new way to grasp what he's getting at (202), and to realize he's been earning and learning that cold eye for a lifetime.

I remember at some point, probably when I was in college, reading a most likely apocryphal story about Thomas Hardy, which I have since been unable to track down, despite repeated efforts, which makes me wonder if I just made it up for my own comfort. In any case, it went something like this: A very young (I'm thinking maybe three or four years old) Thomas Hardy is found crying inconsolably on the back steps. I'm not sure by whom. But this person asks him what could be making him so sad at such a young age. He looks up and says: "Because I know what this life is going to be like." Hardy turned out to be a most magnificent opposite of Monty Python's Eric Idle, hanging on the cross next to Brian in Monty Python's *The Life of Brian*. For Hardy, it was "Always look on the *dark* side of life." I respect Hardy for that. He was true to his vision. And I sympathize with his premonition. One of the legends about me in our family history is that I cried almost continuously for the whole first year of my life. There is a wealth of supporting detail for this story—including doctor's testimony—to persuade me that it is essentially true. I was gaunt and pale, tinged bluish, and wailed night and day. As the story goes, on my first birthday, I stopped crying and, as far as anyone knew, I never cried again. That's not true, of course, the last part, though when I have since then, I try to do it alone. In any case, when I read this story about Hardy I decided to understand my own apparent misery as an infant as rooted in the same insight: we spend some hard time here and we're here for a while. A little upset at the outset is warranted; then buck up and get on with it. A dry eye may not be a cold eye, but it's a start.

One way of doing that is, as Whitman recommends, to be "both in and out of the game," coming up for a breath for a few seconds with the ineffable. This is a form of "ecstasy" in the most practical and routine sense of that word, not as extreme and sustained as Whitman's by any means, just a quick step outside the system, a moment of stasis, and then back. For me, the time I must spend "in the game" is fine; but it's the time out of it that makes it all work.

☙

"A LIFE CONSUMED BY SILENCE" . . . that was the headline that garnished page one of the *Pittsburgh Post-Gazette* on April 22, 2007, just a few days after the horrific, murderous events on the Virginia Tech campus. The term "consumed" here has multiple negative valences associated with it that need not be detailed to be clear. The story itself begins with a poignant account of the frustration of Seung Hui Cho's mother with her son's persistently "meek" behavior during his youth. The seemingly submissive attitude that supported this behavior is characterized as a "silence," in which he was "buried," one that she wishes now he had been able to break, thereby leaving him "transformed." The implication of course is that if not for that silence the story would have reached a decidedly better outcome.

A similar set of metaphors frames John Berryman's *Dream Songs*. In the opening poem, Henry's problem is characterized this way:

> Huffy Henry hid   the day,
> unappeasable Henry sulked.
> I see his point,—a trying to put things over.
> It was the thought that they thought
> they could *do* it made Henry wicked & away.
> But he should have come out and talked. (*DS* 3)

The day that Henry hid, we find out in the book's penultimate poem, is buried with his father, "who shot his heart out in a Florida dawn" (*DS* 406). Death and destruction haunt the intervening poems. At one point Henry even fears he has committed a murder of his own, concluding that wasn't true only because: "he went over everyone, & nobody's missing. / Often he reckons, in the dawn, them up. / Nobody is ever missing" (33). Again, the implication is that if only Henry had "come out and talked" sooner or more or better, his fate, too, would have been a happier one. There are, I'm sure, many sources and causes for the horrors in these stories. I just don't believe that silence is the main one.

I've been writing about my own self-enforced silences at key junctures in the progress along my writerly path. These silences have been quite productive for me. They have to some extent produced rather than consumed the life I have led in their shelter, both my own and the one I share with the poets who join me there. Language can, obviously, accomplish many things, but "talk" in and of itself, no matter Henry's situation, is no panacea for resolving our inmost problems or dilemmas (or, for that matter, most of the vast array of public problems that afflict our workplaces, our world). John Berryman's biography is ample evidence of just that. In the *Dream Songs*, Henry, that thinly veiled, mildly comic, stand-in for Berryman himself actually does come out and talk. A lot. Repeatedly. Manically. Brilliantly. Beautifully. At the end, all Henry is able to do is "moan and rave," "scrabble . . . right down" into this "dreadful banker's grave" and "ax the casket open" (406) in a paroxysm of rage. As for Berryman, who one might argue should be the ultimate beneficiary of this long, potentially therapeutic sojourn through Henry's "plights and gripes" (16), it didn't work out so well for him, either. I remember writing a review of his *Love and Fame* for *Best Seller*s in 1971. He concludes that book with a moving series of "Eleven Addresses to the Lord," a set of simple, elegant prayers that, I thought, and probably wrote (I can't find the review itself) indexed a deep peace of mind, full of both humility and resolve, as if the "roiling & babbling & braining" (40) of the *Dream Songs* had been brought to their proper rest, all that talking having finally paid off. A few months later Berryman jumped to his death from a bridge. So much for coming out and talking, I thought, as I wrote the elegy I offered above.

It may seem odd that I am delivering an appeal for some now and then silences at the end of a book full of all this "talking" about poetry (that other kind of talking) and its great value. Or that I write here about writing poems to inaugurate periods of silence that have always been followed, sooner or later, by other long stretches of talking. Easy to say, you might be saying, after (rather than before) all that I want to say has already been said. Why valorize the inevitable break in the noise as anything more than the simple, human need to rest?

Good point. All I can say is this: This is not a book that seeks to promote anyone's coming out and talking for its own sake, especially my own. Quite the contrary. Everything I write about here was consummated in some sort of silence. I read the words on the page silently and responded in silence. Or I read the words on the page aloud, thereby silencing my own urge to fill up the stillness they came graciously to occupy. And this book does not, finally, urge you to listen to my talking as if that is its ultimate value, or even simply to do what I've done with the few poets who have turned out to be important for me. It invites you to find those conversations of your own that can actually help you with your life and to pursue them in a silent space that is not entirely of your own making or the making of those you have invited in to share it with you. These important transactions take place, often, in solitude and usually without sound, as one sits and engages, in an interactive way, with an interlocutor who, in saying silently the same thing over and over, says something brand new each and every time. And when the conversations stop, as they must, there is a silence left behind that is entirely different from the one that was there beforehand. This is not a life consumed by silence, promoting death. This is a silence infused with life, promoting . . .

I have been trying for days now to utter that elusive "ultimate word," but it's just not happening. Every time I try to put a word in that spot it dies off before I finish typing it. Or the opposite, it starts to breed other words, like a bacterium dividing and dividing until the silence is fully colonized. That's what words do. They generate others. But to do what they do best, they need also to be stopped. As Whitman says in one of his many paroxysms of "speech," midway through "Song of Myself":

> My voice goes after what my eyes cannot reach.
> With the twirl of my tongue I encompass worlds and volumes of
>   worlds. (57, 566–67)

But he immediately warns himself:

> Come now I will not be tantalized . . . . you conceive too much of
>   articulation. (57, 571)

Likewise, Wordsworth writes and writes and writes, but there are still all the thoughts that "lie too deep for tears," which are beyond words but can only come into being, for him and for us, because of the words that surround them, defining the boundaries around their unbreakable silences. That is one of the things—what he can't say and knows he can't say—that makes Wordsworth so appealing to Mill, who is looking for a space to stand in alongside a companionable spirit, not ensconced in the heart of his darkness, but abiding by its borders. Even the mariner, a big-time talker, tells his tale because he is "forced" to, in order to relieve the "agony" that burns periodically within his heart. But really, for the mariner, "tis sweeter far . . . to walk together . . . with a goodly company" after the talk is all over, as it is for me to walk together with my wife, in our sometimes silence. Maybe the mariner should, as his story closes, have just kept his mouth shut instead of adding the disputable moral tag. But words have a lot of momentum. They can be hard to stop. They need to be, at least for a while, every now and then.

I have wanted, following Mill, to make a case for the poet who doesn't, even can't, write poems, a contradiction that makes perfect sense to me. The role of the poet is open for everyone, not just the writers of poems and most especially not just for the famous writers of poems. In some situations, one actually *becomes* a poet by resisting rather than acceding to the words that swoop in unbidden and consume the moment in their swirl. How can that be, I ask again.

I think of my original "forethoughtful query," the one that has been going before me as I wrote this book, just like Coleridge's "invisible guardian and guide:" What is poetry good for? Certainly, for me, it's been good for all of the things I've talked about so far: hearing a companionable voice at a difficult moment, thinking through some complex life problems, addressing pressing philosophical questions, getting a job I enjoy, connecting me with other great works in many fields, writing poems of my own and writing scholarship, including this book. But above all, I'm thinking now, it has gotten me through the words and back out into an abiding silence that is richer and fuller for my having broken it for a while. It is not the absence of words but a presence surrounded by them, after they pass. I could not enter that realm in such a way had I not read and re-read all of those poets. That's why we read and re-read a lot of things: not just to "get" them, but to get *beyond* them, a little further than they take us, not just into Larissa but out of it, on the other side, where we can open ourselves toward something else, something more. This is what poetry is good for: not the ultimate word, but what's just beyond it . . . now.

❧ Epilogue

I realized while I was writing the final chapter—as my own "life of the author" began to emerge through my poems as a subject for inquiry in much the same way as the other poets I am talking about—that my "defense of poetry" is not complete without some sampling of my creative work. The main difficulty is how to do it. I have written poems on and off for forty years and I have lots of them, with themes and styles that vary significantly from one "era" to the next. So I've been trying to find a more inventive angle into this part of the project.

A few days ago I was out walking in the woods—it was mid-January, about fifteen degrees, a few inches of new snow, blue sky, just beautiful. I was alone that day, thinking, for some reason, about what it was like walking in the woods when I was a boy growing up in Forest City, Pennsylvania, animated by an inner energy that generated an excited self-delightedness, not unlike the one Wordsworth describes so often. And all of a sudden it struck me that I felt at that moment just like I did back then. This realization was exhilarating—because when you make it past sixty, I thought, without having had that inner spark extinguished by the rigors of all that life, well, what could be better than that? One of the nice things about nature is it makes no judgments, delivers no advice or criticism, pretty much no matter how oddly you act around it, which is why I like it so much. It puts me entirely at ease, and I can be myself, which in this case meant I could laugh unabashedly for a good part of the rest of my walk. That's how happy I was. Along the way, I started doing what I often do when I feel at home with myself: remembering my own poems and reciting them in my head. The one that came up first that day was a dark and turbulent one I wrote in the late 1970s or early 1980s. It's called "Missing Americans:"

> Bearded, sweaty, he crouches in the shade
> leafing through the August *Penthouse.*
> I buy a dozen daisies from him, pretending
> the day is lovely, there is romance
> where I'm going, a woman in the flesh.
> As I turn the corner a wall of heat
> heaves up from the street. I stroll
> slowly through it, pretending I am
> Norman Vincent Peale afloat on an iceberg.
> It doesn't work. I am too hot to think
> straight, might as well be Buffalo Bob
> layered in braided suede, or Howdy
> Doody, wooden headed and sweatless.
>
> They say the weather is going crazy.
> El Niño swirls slowly off the coast of Peru.
> Molten lava oozes down a swollen Hawaiian
> hillside. A year's worth of rain falls
> in a weekend on Galveston. The Sudan
> turns Sahara. And I am only halfway
> home. Norman Vincent Peale is lost at sea.
> His ice cube clinks inside a glass.
> Clarabell steals a Jeep in El Salvador.
> Four women fall to their knees pleading,
> el niño, el niño, just a kid, shoots them
> to keep cool. I stroll slowly home alone,
> a dozen daisies wilting in my fist.

The poem is based on an actual walk home from work, and all the references are to events in the news of that week. It's an odd poem to step forward at a moment of such self-satisfaction, all that violence and heat. But what struck me most vividly, for the first time really, were the poem's daisies. Why would someone with no one to go home to buy a dozen daisies as if he did? Well, I thought, why not? That's a pretty good summary statement for why I write poems, too. I'll leave it to you to work out the details, and implications, of that comparison.

That's where I start this set of selections from my life as a poet, with flowers, which crop up over and over in my work, serving many different purposes, as they do for so many poets. Here's one, for example, from the "Morning Song" series I draw on for the bluebird poem in chapter 4:

> This morning
> I woke to
> a roomful of azaleas,
> thousands of them, clouds
> of flowers blooming ferociously,
> more gorgeous than I
> could ever hope to afford,
> enough lush color to crowd out
> even my loudest dreams.
>
> I lolled for a while
> in a haze of fragrances too
> hothouse sweet to breathe.
> Then I hacked my way
> to the stairs thinking:
> sometimes you cannot trust
> anything to be
> only reasonably beautiful.
>
> On my way to work I saw nothing
> except the fog of my hot
> breath catching itself like
> cotton on the frost-
> sharp air and I thought
> of all I had meant
> to say that day about
> my being beautiful
> and wouldn't now because of
> those damn azaleas.

Here's one from the late 1980s with a more somber aspect—a nice, messy mix of losses—called "The Taste of Water":

> These days when I think of you
> it is like remembering the taste of water

from an empty glass.
I know I drank from it
this afternoon, while I was working
sweat-drenched and achy in the garden
to plant the rose bushes
I got from my father over the weekend
because he is in the hospital now,
unable to turn the earth
by himself for at least another month,
too long to let those roses sit
in their tight pots, waiting.

On the long drive home, uncertain of what I'd find,
I tried to remember how things went wrong with us
and couldn't. My mother and I joked about divorce
over dinner. It has finally come to that.

I have no idea how love can be reduced
to nothing.
But it is. Every day.
By all of us.
I am a witness.

All I can think to tell you is that today,
the hottest day in a couple of years here,
I spent part of my afternoon
digging holes for my father's rose bushes.
They are important to me for reasons
I have no interest in exploring.
My children run back and forth squealing
through the lawn sprinkler.
Sweat mats my hair and streams down my face,
which I think is smiling.
I have survived what I've had to,
as most of us do, most of the time,
until thirst is simply there again,
waiting to be quenched.

This one is from a little series of "Spring Songs" I wrote in the mid-1990s:

A tiny iris spikes through last night's snow.
I have waited all winter by the window
for this moment. The blossom
opens:
each petal a dark velvet pool,
perfectly still, over which a man rows a boat
slowly, on his way back home.

I am suddenly beside myself, staring
at that strange, pale, gray-haired fellow
standing by the window, waiting for
something.
Before the morning is out, he will be gone,
and there will be only one of us here,
smiling, on his way back home.

Even in tundra, there can be flowers. Here is poem III from a chapbook-length series of poems I wrote in the late 1970s under the title *Snow Man*:

It went hard out there
for the flowers: flash-
card blurs of red dashing
past breathless upstarts
of yellow spattering
freak summer snow-thins;
pale pink, pale blue
pastel woozies bobbing
through thaw fogs
prickled by sunlight
still stiff from winter
and stiffening already
toward winter again.
A cold world for color
to go on coloring in.

Lucky.
He hadn't a mind now
for color.
He came to see snow-sheets

billowing up like bear thighs,
horizonless white
steaming out of infinity.

He courted each flake
kissing bittersweet
on his cheek, unballed
his tight little fists,
limbered fingers into
each hexagonal hole
lifting back the delicate
tissue until his whole
head bobbed through
and he knew where
he was and what he had
found and a thrill
of guilt throbbed
in his throat
puffed up the muggy
steam-pots of his cheeks
tickled his quick
hot tongue until
the gentle rhythms
of snowflakes contracting
over and over slowly
into infinity pumped
voice-box wonders
out of his mouth like
words.

One last flower poem before I move on, the coda poem from a series called "Nine Lives." It follows eight darkly comic portraits of different women in relation to the same vague, amorphous male presence, which are based on time spent observing couples-at-odds, some of which included me, in bars and clubs in the early 1980s:

Crazy
as the wind he was and wanted,
for himself, nothing; but for her:

the most glorious chrysanthemums,
armloads of yellow held loose, huge
blooms oozing dollops of sunlight;
behind them, his smile, so wide
no one, not even her, could ever hope
to resist; then he'd run toward her
through the tall grass, in slo-mo
maybe, his dozens of chrysanthemums
bobbing every which way, crazy
as the wind he was, and wanted.

Or so he told his florist in the morning,
who recommended roses, or a nosegay—
anything but crazy, but chrysanthemums,
but what he wanted, was: the wind.

Flowers will get you only so far, of course. These next three poems explore some of the ironies of mid-life. They're from the early/mid 1990s:

LIMBO ROCK

The lines for the water slides seem to snake away for days.
Sleek, brown bodies steam dry between rides.
Their parents, pink lumps slumped into inner tubes,
bump lazily down a curvy turquoise culvert.

It must be a hundred degrees today, even under this tree.
I creep deeper into the mottled shade, crocodile out of water.
I can hardly breathe.
"The Limbo Rock" rollicks down from the boardwalk:
"Every limbo boy and girl / All around the limbo world . . ."
Overhead the trees gyrate wildly
in the rising heat, trying, as I am, to reach
the cool languor of autumn, the freedom to let go.

I try to picture "a limbo moon above."
It comes out electric blue, a black plastic sky
oozing away from its wavy-hot edges.
I try to imagine what it is like to "fall in limbo love."
I think it is something I am too old for
but would like to try.

Through the hazy heat I see a thin, lithe boy, tanned deep,
Leaning back, knees bent, duck-stepping up to the limbo stick.
"How low can you go?"
I wish suddenly I were 16 again.
Or at least had worn my bathing suit today.
This must be just what these leaves will be thinking about
in October, on their way down to the cool, beautiful ground,
wishing it were August again, that they could gyrate
wildly one last time in the unbearable heat.

I head out into the sun.
Sweat soaks my shirt.
My daughter has been splashing around in the crowded pool.
Now she runs to me, shivering, her lips blue.
I swoop down and scoop her up,
my knees buckling under her weight.
Old, young, too hot, too cold,
parents, children, each inching along
in their own separate lines.
Even the leaves in such a big rush
to get where they won't want to be.
On a day like this, if you stop to think about it,
none of it really figures.

My daughter and I sway and laugh
to the last few bars of music:
"All around the limbo clock . . ."
Pretty soon she doesn't shiver
and I don't sweat.
"Hey, let's do the limbo rock."

BREAKING THE ICE

I

Last night's freezing rain slid
like a tight glove—precisely,
down to the finest detail—

over leaf and twig and bud,
each one iridescent now
in the bright March sun.

I've been studying this scene
for the last half hour or so
trying to find a way of saying
how life is sometimes like that.
You know, the ironic play
of fire over ice:
thin, shimmering fingers
straining toward the sun
against all odds, achieving something.
Or the other way around:
slivers of heat intruding
into the good wood
which shivers, gives way.
I can't make either one work.

II

In the ninth grade I prayed
day after day
that she'd stop and talk to me
on her way out of school.
I'd stand by the door
to catch her eye
as she hurried by,
try to craft a clever line
to break the ice.
I couldn't make either one work.

So, every afternoon at three
for the last thirty-five years—
in my mind's eye, at least—
she breezes right by
without noticing I'm there,
hugs her smug boyfriend
climbs aboard the same clunky bus
and chugs away.

III

I walk down to the bus stop
to meet my son.
By the time we get home
the ice is crashing down
in huge slabs that splash
all over the backyard.
We sit on the back steps
and laugh like crazy, amazed
at all that dazzle and disarray.

As his bus heads up the hill
I could swear I see her
looking out the window at us,
big eyes, like it just dawned on her,
that tomorrow,
when she's heading home,
I won't be there.

AUTUMN WALKS TO WORK

I

Maples drench everything
in lovely shades of red.
Always above average,
never stunning, shunning
attention, they display
what is left them, yield
slowly and only to need.

Today, while I am taking
care of my affairs,
I will remind myself:
Maples drench everything
in lovely shades of red.

II

The two elms on Flagstaff Hill,
so lush, so sexual, just yesterday,
went last night—that needling
rain—in privacy, to pieces.
Today: a shambles of yellow
dulling down the lawn.

I know just what it's like,
those all-at-once undressings
in the cold; and the mornings-
after. I shuffle down the leaf-
slick hill, hoping not to slip.

III

Like a team of breaching whales
locked in freeze-frame
at the top of a leap, three sycamores
lean over the street, waiting
for stop-action to start up again:
a splash of sun-bleached
umbers, a settled sea.

Such colors as these, they say, emerge
only as dominant green
recedes: spectacles of absence,
brief celebrations
before loss entire.

IV

Ginkgos—licks of flame
stilled, cool tongues—
line the sidewalk.
The rest of the trees
on the block—coal-black
and alien their remains--
gave up days ago.
Ginkgos still heave back

rain-soaked manes
and menace.

I walk by watching
only out of the corner
of my eye, wanting
not to intrude on
what soon they stand to lose.

I would like to conclude with the closing poem of a twenty-poem chap-book called *Making Book* that I wrote back in the mid-1970s. I had been reading a book by Claude Lévi-Strauss, a French anthropologist, and came across these lines, which became my guiding epigraph for the poems: "Language was born all at once. . . . After a transformation . . . a change has taken place, from a stage where nothing had meaning to a stage where everything had." The image that came immediately into my head was of some pre- or post-historic, pretty happy, un-word-burdened, sap of a guy waking up one morning with all of language fully ensconced and clamoring in his head, and I wrote these lines—"With hair to his feet and a stutter in / his step he hobbled down the mountain / expounding . . ."—which turned soon into a four-stanza, thirty-six-line poem that established the style, tone, and form for the rest of the series. That opening poem ends this way:

This was chaos never done by sun.
He scratched his chin and wondered
at the mess that he was in, climbed
a tree to find out what went wrong.
Peering down from the topmost branch
he observed something ugly and inevitable
lying beneath him on the ground
beating up dust with dirty wings.
He waited for himself to descend.

From there, he "descends" into history. For each subsequent poem I picked a historical epoch and followed my mock-heroic protagonist through it as he tries to recover, through language, the sense of placid equanimity he felt before he got all those words. Each time he comes at his problem with enthusiasm and confidence. Each time, it ends in something ranging between disaster and catastrophe. The poems are full of jokes and allusions to philosophic, religious, mythological, scientific, and artistic texts. The concluding poem is located in the northeast Pennsylvania landscape I grew up in, the stark juxtapositions of timeless natural enclaves and the mid-twentieth-century mess left behind by the railroad and coal-mining industries gone bust. And it's the only one that ends with a glimmer of hope. A nice place to stop.

For Good

Stopped at last in his tracks by the train
of his thought, his wits wafted
off like steam. He wanted
to station himself rail-
straight and stare, the wild-wind-whine
in his ear, at green leaves holding on.
But they flew off, fell down further
and faster than sound, curled up,
crisped, and rotted on the ground.

He took a long look at himself and shook.
He wanted out, went out on his knees
and wept. Trees kept themselves intact
through frost and the fall and he knelt there
on the leaf-fall through the long nights
and all and he knelt there through snowfall
and snowmelt until time came to crawl down
waist deep in leafmeal, chastened and afraid
of all he had come to know by posing

as himself. Then he too fell hard
on his dark luck, burned
black and blacker and blackest
fueling foolish doubts. Forests came
and went, pressed up next to him,
and he lay down with them, waited
to be mined and trucked to breaker, cracked
and picked and sorted, packed and sold,
thick veins gone up in smoke to stem the cold.

His heritage: ashes in a pit,
clinkers caught to clog the grate,

a landscape pocked, scabrous, all a waste.
But one black thought escaped, lay down
in loveliness and slept. Somewhere
in the back of his wildest dream it poked
through bald rock, self-hewn,
multifaceted, brilliant in the light,
a blue-white beacon beckoning his kind.

The poets you decide to read may or may not inspire you to write poems of your own—as I said, I heartily endorse John Stuart Mill's notion that one need not be writing poems to be a fully credentialed poet—but mine did. For the most part, I enjoyed that work immensely and have been enlivened by it. When I didn't or wasn't, I stopped. The writer of those poems, through his words, accompanies me in much the same way as the many other poets I have spent my time getting to know. This process of writing poems tends to get so enmeshed in the mystifications of school and culture that it seems beyond reach, or irrelevant, to most people, out of the range of their interests, inclinations, or skills. Nothing could be further from the truth. People make beautiful things out of all kinds of materials. The advantage of words is they are always with us and they're free for us to use in any way we wish. That's about all you need to know to start turning them into poems. Believe me, I know.

❧ Works Cited

Abrams, M. H. *The Mirror and the Lamp: Romantic Theory and the Critical Tradition.* New York: Oxford University Press, 1953.

Auden, W. H. "In Memory of W. B. Yeats." *Collected Poems.* New York: Modern Library/Random House, 2007.

Augustine. *The Confessions: Basic Writings of Saint Augustine.* Ed. Whitney J. Oates. New York: Random House, 1948.

Bakhtin, Mikhail M. *The Dialogic Imagination: Four Essays.* Ed. Michael Holquist. Trans. Caryl Emerson and Michael Holquist. Austin: University of Texas Press, 1981.

Barthes, Roland. "The Death of the Author." *Image, Music, Text.* Trans. Stephen Heath. New York: Hill and Wang/Farrar, Straus and Giroux, 1977.

Berryman, John. *The Dream Songs.* New York: Farrar, Straus and Giroux, 1969.

———. *Love and Fame.* New York: Farrar, Straus and Giroux, 1970.

Blake, William. *The Norton Anthology of English Literature.* New York: Norton, 1968.

Bly, Robert. *Leaping Poetry.* Boston: Beacon Press, 1972.

Burke, Kenneth. *The Philosophy of Literary Form.* Berkeley: University of California Press, 1941.

Burns, Robert. "To a Mouse." *English Romantic Writers.* Ed. David Perkins. New York: Harcourt Brace, 1995.

Carlyle, Thomas. *Life of John Sterling: Latter-Day Pamphlets.* Vol. 13. New York: Peter Fenelon Collier, 1897.

———. *Reminiscences.* Vol. II. London: Longmans, Green and Co., 1881.

Coleridge, Samuel Taylor. *Biographia Literaria.* London: George Bell and Sons, 1884.

———. "The Rime of the Ancient Mariner." *English Romantic Writers.* Ed. David Perkins. New York: Harcourt Brace, 1995.

———. *The Works of Samuel Taylor Coleridge: Prose and Verse.* Philadelphia: Thomas, Cowperthwaite, 1840.

Crane, Stephen. *The Black Riders and Other Lines.* Boston: Copeland and Day, 1896.

Eigner, Larry. *The World and Its Streets, Places.* Santa Barbara: Black Sparrow, 1977.

Eliot, T. S. *Poems 1909–1925.* Faber and Gwyer, London, 1925, 123.

———. *The Sacred Wood.* New York: Methuen and Co., 1920.

———. *The Waste Land.* New York : Boni and Liveright, 1922.

Emerson, Ralph Waldo, *Selected Writings of Ralph Waldo Emerson.* New York: Signet/Penguin, 1965.

Flint, F. S. "Imagisme." *Poetry* 1.6 (March 1913): 198.

Foucault, Michel. *Discourse on Thinking.* Trans. John M. Anderson and E. Hans Freund. New York: Harper, 1966.

———. "What Is an Author?" *The Foucault Reader.* Ed. Paul Rabinow. New York: Pantheon Books, 1984, 101–20.

Hazlitt, William. *English Romantic Writers.* Ed. David Perkins. New York: Harcourt Brace, 1995.

Heidegger, Martin. *Being and Time.* Trans. John Macquarrie and Edward Robinson. San Francisco: Harper, 1962.

Kamccn, Paul. "Autumn Walks to Work." *5 AM* 6 (1993): n.p.

———. "For Daphne on the Mornings After." *Brownstone Review* 1 (Summer 1995): 12–14.

———. "For Good." *Poet Lore* 74.2 (Summer 1979): 73.

———. "Limbo Rock." *Gulf Stream Review* 6 (1992): 66–68.

———. "Missing Americans." *Gulf Stream Review* 2 (1990): 19.

———. "Morning Song 4." *West Branch* 24 (1989): 123.

———. "Morning Song 3." *Piedmont Literary Review* 10.1 (1985): 123.

———. "Nine Lives: Coda" *Boston Literary Review* 2 (1985): n.p.

————. "Reading Poets." *Georgia Review* 35.4 (Winter 1981): 775–78.

————. "Spring Song, #2." *PoetryMagazine.com* (June 2002).

————. "The Taste of Water." *Endless Mountains Review* (Winter 1997): 9.

————. *Writing/Teaching: Essays Toward a Rhetoric of Pedagogy*. Pittsburgh: University of Pittsburgh Press, 2000.

Knierim, Thomas. "Parmenides and Zeno." *The Big View*. www.thebigview. com/greeks/parmenides.html (accessed January 10, 2008).

Mill, John Stuart. "Thoughts on Poetry and Its Varieties." *Dissertations and Discussions, Political, Philosophical and Historical*. Vol. I. New York: Henry Holt and Co., 1873.

Olson, Charles. *Selected Writings*. New York: New Directions, 1966.

Parmenides. *Parmenides and Empedocles: The Fragments in Verse Translation*. Trans. Stanley Lombardo. San Francisco: Grey Fox Press. 1979.

Plath, Sylvia. *Ariel*. New York: Harper and Row, 1965.

Plato. *The Collected Dialogues of Plato*. Ed. Edith Hamilton and Huntingdon Cairns. New York: Pantheon Books, 1961.

Poe, Edgar Allan. *The Works of Edgar Allan Poe*. Ed. Rufus Wilmot Griswold. New York: J. S. Redfield, 1850.

Pound, Ezra. "A Few Don'ts by an *Imagiste*." *Poetry* 1.6 (March 1913). Reprinted in "A Retrospect" in *Pavannes and Divisions*. New York: Alfred A. Knopf, 1918 (page numbers refer to this edition).

————. "In a Station of the Metro." *Poetry* 2 (April 1913): 1.

————. *Lustra*. London: William Clowes and Sons, 1916.

————. "Vorticism." *Fortnightly Review* 571 (Sept. 1, 1914): 461–71.

Ree, Jonathan. *Heidegger*. New York: Routledge, 1999.

Richards, I. A. *Practical Criticism: A Study of Literary Judgment*. New York: Harvest Books/Harcourt, 1929.

Rosenthal, M. L. "Poetry as Confession." *Nation*, Sept. 1959: 109–12.

Schreiner, Olive. *Story of an African Farm*. New York: Penguin Classics, 1982.

Snyder, Gary. *The Gary Snyder Reader*. Washington D.C.: Counterpoint, 1999.

————. *Paris Review* 141 (Winter 1966). Reprinted in *The Gary Snyder Reader*, 322–38.

Whitman, Walt. *Leaves of Grass: The First (1855) Edition*. New York: Penguin Books, 2005.

Williams, William Carlos. *The Autobiography of William Carlos Williams*. New York: New Directions, 1967.

————. *Imaginations*. New York: New Directions, 1970.

————. *Paterson*. New York: New Directions, 1963.

Wimsatt, William, and Monroe Beardsley. *The Verbal Icon: Studies in the Meaning of Poetry*. Lexington: University of Kentucky Press, 1954.

Wordsworth, William. "Ode: Intimations of Immortality from Recollections of Early Childhood." *English Romantic Writers*. Ed. David Perkins. New York: Harcourt Brace, 1995.

Wordsworth, William, and Samuel Taylor Coleridge. *Lyrical Ballads, with a Few Other Poems*. Bristol: Printed by Briggs and Cottle for T. N. Longman, 1798.

Wright, James. *Collected Poems*. Middletown, Conn.: Wesleyan University Press, 1972.

Yeats, William Butler. *Selected Poems and Four Plays*. New York: Scribner, 1996.

❧ Index